SCHOLASTIC
Spelling™

Louisa Moats and Barbara Foorman

Welcome!

COVER CREDITS: Illustrations: snowflake: CSA Archive; stamp, fish: Stephen Foster; rocket: Bill Mayer; (back cover) rhino: Vince Andriani. Photography: bl: © Susan Richman for Scholastic Inc.; mr: © Alastair Black/Tony Stone Images; br: © Ana Esperanza Nance for Scholastic Inc.; tc: Images © PhotoDisc,Inc.

ILLUSTRATION: pp. 9, 13, 16, 19, 23, 24, 26, 27, 28, 29, 37, 39, 40, 41, 43, 44, 45, 49, 52, 53, 56, 57, 61, 68, 72, 73, 76, 80, 84, 92, 93, 96, 100, 103, 104, 105, 108, 116, 117, 158, 159, 160, 161, 162, 164, 165, 166, 167, 168, 169, 170, 171, 174, 175, 176, 178, Lookout Word, Spelling Strategy pages, pencil and computer icons: John Margeson. pp. 77, 120, 121, 124, 127, 129, 133, 137, 141, 145, 148, 151, 155, 156, 159, 160, 161, 173, 175, 177: Tim Haggerty. p. 45: Rita Lascaro. Rhino Character, Spelling Sleuth Cat, Memory Jogger Rabbit: Vince Andriani. All children's art: Matthew R. Geiger.

PHOTOGRAPHY: p. 8tl: © David S. Waitz for Scholastic Inc. p. 12tl: © Francis Clark Westfield for Scholastic Inc. p. 16tl: © Ana Esperanza Nance for Scholastic Inc.; p. 17tc: © Stanley Bach for Scholastic Inc.; tl: © Ana Esperanza Nance for Scholastic Inc.; tl: © Bie Bostrom for Scholastic Inc.; tc: Images ©1996 PhotoDisc, Inc.; tl: © John Lei for Scholastic Inc.; tc: © Sharon Chester/Comstock Inc. p. 20tl: © Clara Von Aich for Scholastic Inc. p. 24tl: © Francis Clark Westfield for Scholastic Inc. p. 25ml: © David S. Waitz for Scholastic Inc.; c: © Francis Clark Westfield. p. 25bc: © Bie Bostrom for Scholastic Inc.; ml: © Zig Leszczynski/Animals Animals; c: © Renee Lynn/Tony Stone Images. p. 31br: © Stanley Bach for Scholastic Inc. p. 32tl: © Richard Lee for Scholastic Inc. p. 33tl: © David S. Waitz for Scholastic Inc.; others: ©.Ana Esperanza Nance for Scholastic Inc. p. 36: © Ana Esperanza Nance for Scholastic Inc. p. 40tl: © Ken Karp for Scholastic Inc. p. 44tl: © Scott Campbell for Scholastic Inc. p. 48tl: © John Lei for Scholastic Inc. p. 55br: © Stanley Bach for Scholastic Inc. p. 56: © David Lawrence for Scholastic Inc. p. 60tl: © Scott Campbell for Scholastic Inc. p. 64tl: © Steven Gottlieb/FPG International. p. 68tl: © John Lei for Scholastic Inc. tl: © Richard Megna for Scholastic Inc. p. 72tl: © Diane Padys /FPG International. p. 79br: © Stanley Bach for Scholastic Inc. p. 80tl: © Clara Von Aich for Scholastic Inc. p. 84tl: © David S. Waitz for Scholastic Inc. p. 88tl: © David S.Waitz for Scholastic Inc. p. 92tl: © Gary Buss/FPG International. p. 96tl: © Koji Kitagawa/Superstock. p. 103br: © Julie Gottesman for Scholastic Inc. p. 104tl: © Grant Huntington for Scholastic Inc. p. 108tl: © Francis Clark Westfield for Scholastic Inc. p. 109tc: © Scott Campbell for Scholastic Inc.; tc: © David S. Waitz for Scholastic Inc. p. 111bc: © David S. Waitz for Scholastic Inc.; bl: © Chris Trayer for Scholastic Inc.; bc: © Grant Huntington for Scholastic Inc.; bc: © A. Schmidecker/FPG International; bc: © Enrique Cubillo for Scholastic Inc.; bl: © Dennie Eagleson for Scholastic Inc.; bl: © Francis Clark Westfield for Scholastic Inc.; bl: © John Lei for Scholastic Inc.; bc: Images ©1996 PhotoDisc, Inc. p. 112tl: © Francis Clark Westfield for Scholastic Inc. p. 113c: © Grant Huntington for Scholastic Inc.; tc: © George DiSario/The Stock Market; tc: © Ralph A. Reinhold/Animals, Animals; c: © J.Pickerell/FPG International; c: Images ©1996 PhotoDisc, Inc. p. 116tl: © David S. Waitz for Scholastic Inc. p. 120tl: © Stanley Bach for Scholastic Inc. p. 128tl: © John Lei for Scholastic Inc. p. 132tl: © John Curry for Scholastic Inc. p. 136tl: © Ana Esperanza Nance for Scholastic Inc. p. 140: © Ana Esperanza Nance for Scholastic Inc. p. 144tl: © The Stock Market. p. 151br: © Stanley Bach for Scholastic Inc. p. 159tc: © Anup & Manos Shah for Scholastic Inc. p. 166mr: © Mickey Gibson/Animals Animals. p. 170bc: © Enrique Cubillo for Scholastic Inc. p. 173tc: © David S. Waitz for Scholastic inc. p. 174br: © C. Prescott Allen/Animals Animals. p. 175br: © Bie Bostrom for Scholastic Inc.

Contents

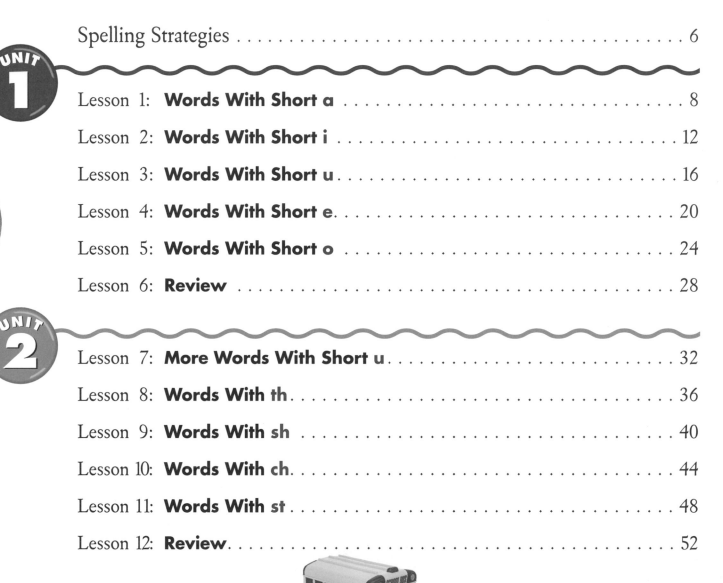

Contents

Contents

Spelling Strategies
Word Study Path

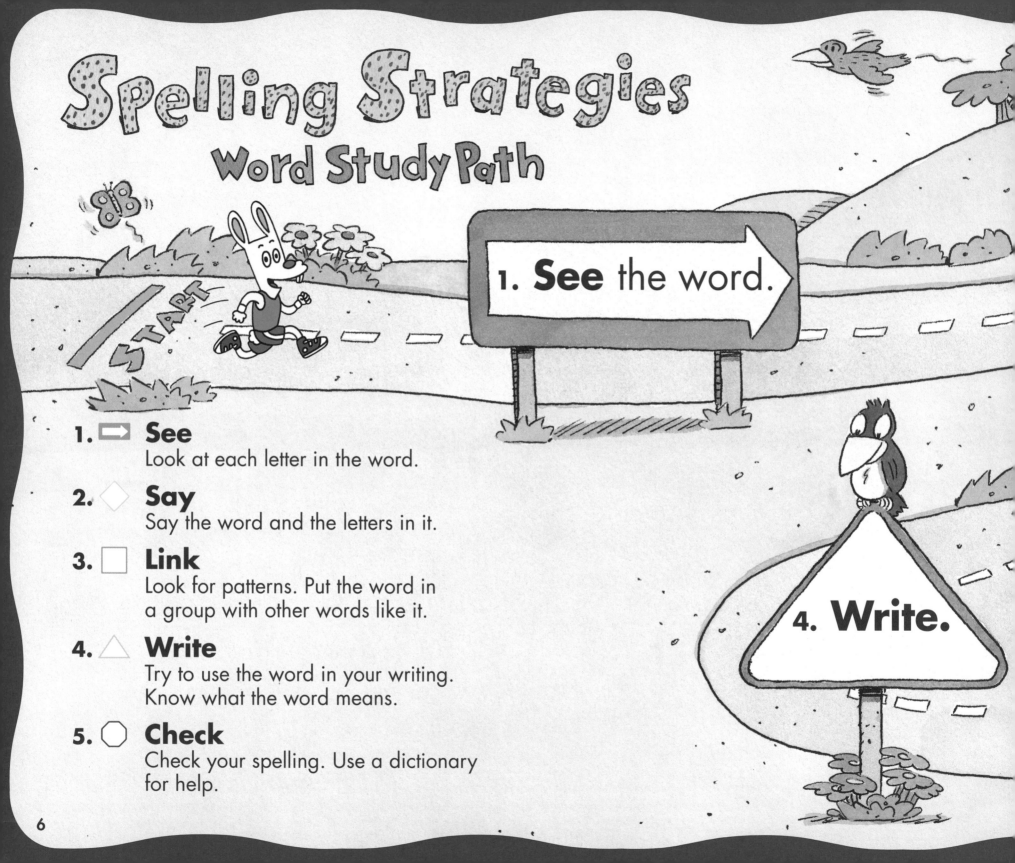

1. See the word.

1. ➡ **See**
   Look at each letter in the word.

2. ◇ **Say**
   Say the word and the letters in it.

3. ☐ **Link**
   Look for patterns. Put the word in a group with other words like it.

4. △ **Write**
   Try to use the word in your writing. Know what the word means.

5. ⬡ **Check**
   Check your spelling. Use a dictionary for help.

4. Write.

2. **Say** it slowly.

3. **Link** sounds and letters.

5. **Check.**

Spelling Words

am	hand
as	land
ask	mad
has	add
act	was *LOOKOUT WORD*

Review	Challenge
been	camp
mine	grass
had	

My Words

Words With Short a

A **See and Say**

am   mad
ask   hand

These words have the short a sound.
This vowel sound is spelled with the letter a.

Remember this!
Was is **saw**
spelled the
other way.

Memory Jogger

B **Link Sounds and Letters**
Sort the spelling words. Write them on the lines.

a _ _

1. _____
2. _____
3. _____

a _

4. _____
5. _____

_ a _

8. _____
9. _____
10. _____

_ a _ _

6. _____
7. _____

C **Write and Check**
Read the button. Write the two spelling words with the
short **a** sound.

11. _____   12. _____

Say it five
times fast!
Ask Al to add
Ann to the
band.

Ⓐ Make New Words

Change the underlined letter in each word to make a
spelling word. Write the word.

1. <u>i</u>s _____

2. <u>g</u>as _____

3. a<u>n</u>d _____

4. a<u>t</u> _____

5. <u>b</u>and _____

6. ha<u>t</u> _____

7. m<u>u</u>d _____

8. a<u>n</u>t _____

9. ha<u>r</u>d _____

10. as<u>h</u> _____

Ⓑ Add -ed

Add **-ed** to tell about something that already
happened.

land + ed = landed

Write these words with **-ed**.

11. act _____   12. ask _____   13. add _____

Be a Spelling Sleuth

Look at signs for two words
with the short a sound, such
as **cat** or **band**.

SPELL CHAT

Ask a friend to
change a letter in a
spelling word to make
a new word.

Spelling Words	
am	hand
as	land
ask	mad
has	add
act	was

Name ....

Spelling Words

am	hand
as	land
ask	mad
has	add
act	was

Review	Challenge
been	camp
mine	grass
had	

My Words

Quick Write

Write a question about a camp you would like to go to. Use one or more spelling words.

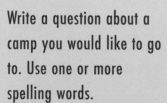

A Write Questions

You are going to a new camp. Write two questions you could ask someone who went there last year. Use two or more spelling words.

You may do this activity on a computer.

1. _____

2. _____

B Proofread

Tad wrote these questions to his friend. He found two mistakes. Find four more mistakes that Tad made, and fix them.

Tip
Remember to begin each sentence with a capital letter. Always end a question with a question mark.

Was
1. Wuz camp fun?

2. Is it as nice az Lakeside Camp?

3. Which camp hed more campers

4. Did they ad a pool?

Now proofread your questions. Check your spelling. Did you begin each sentence with a capital letter? Did you put a question mark at the end of each question?

PROOFREADING MARKS

∧ Add
◯ Check spelling
— Cross out
≡ Capital letter

Study and Review

Name ....

A Use ABC Order

Write the letters that come before and after each letter.

1. ____ d ____

2. ____ m ____

3. ____ h ____

4. ____ s ____

5. ____ u ____

6. ____ o ____

B Test Yourself

Write spelling words by filling in the missing letters.

7. m⬜

8. l⬜⬜

9. ⬜m

10. ⬜a⬜

11. a⬜⬜

12. ⬜⬜k

13. a⬜

14. ⬜a⬜

15. a⬜⬜

16. ⬜a⬜

Get Word Wise

Do you ever say you have your **hands** full? That means you're really busy!

For Tomorrow

➡️ See the word.

◇ Say it slowly.

☐ Link sounds and letters.

▽ Write.

⬡ Check.

Share What short a words did you find?

Spelling Words	
am	hand
as	land
ask	mad
has	add
act	was

Spelling Words

if	miss
gift	fix
lift	mix
him	six
milk	this

LOOKOUT WORD

Review	Challenge
was	little
say	picnic
sit	

My Words

Words With Short i

A **See and Say**   gift   him
milk   fix

These words have the short i sound.
This vowel sound is spelled with the letter i.

Don't miss the second **s** in mis**s**.

Memory Jogger

B **Link Sounds and Letters**
Sort the spelling words. Write them on the lines.

_ i _
1. _____
2. _____
3. _____
4. _____

i _
5. _____

_ _ i _
6. _____

_ i _ _
7. _____
8. _____
9. _____
10. _____

C **Write and Check**
Read the riddle. Write the two spelling words.

11. _____   12. _____

Riddle
Mix cows and ducks. What do you get?
Milk with quackers.

Name ....

A Words That Mean the Same
Write a spelling word to finish each sentence.

1. If you give it, it's a _____ .

2. If you pick it up, you _____ it.

3. If you stir it, you _____ it.

4. If it breaks, you must _____ it.

B Make New Words
Change the last letter in each word to make a
spelling word. Write the word.

5. hit _____   7. is _____

6. sit _____   8. mill _____

Add a letter to the beginning and end of each word
to write a spelling word.

9. ___ i ___   11. ___ is ___

10. ___ hi ___   12. ___ if ___

Be a Spelling Sleuth
Look in a book for two words
with the short i sound, such
as **him** and **this**.

SPELL CHAT

Ask a friend to tell
you the number
for five plus one.

Spelling Words

if	miss
gift	fix
lift	mix
him	six
milk	this

Name . . . .

Spelling Words

if	miss
gift	fix
lift	mix
him	six
milk	this

Review	Challenge
was	little
say	picnic
sit	

My Words

Quick Write ✏️

What if you moved away?
Write what you would miss
most in your town or city.
Use one or more spelling
words.

You may do this activity
on a computer.

Ⓐ Write Facts for a Poster

Make a poster for a trading-card show. Tell
when and where the show will be. Use two or
more spelling words.

Ⓑ Proofread

Kim made this poster about a trading-card show at
her school. She found two mistakes. Find four more
mistakes that Kim made, and fix them.

THIS
DON'T MIS ⟨THISS⟩!

Trading-Card Show

When—Friday, April 8 at 4 o'clock

Where—Little falls School

6 Penny lane

Bring home a gifd.

Wuz at 4 o'clock, now at 5 o'clock!

Tip
Remember to begin
a place name with
a capital letter.

PROOFREADING MARKS

∧ Add
◯ Check spelling
— Cross out
≡ Capital letter

Now proofread your poster. Check your
spelling. Make sure you used a capital letter
to start each place name.

Name ....

A Use ABC Order
Write the missing letters.

1. b ___ d ___ ___ ___ ___

3. ___ ___ l ___ n ___

2. v ___ ___ ___ ___ z

4. r ___ ___ ___ u ___

B Test Yourself
Put the letters in 1-2-3 order to make a spelling word.
Then write the word.

5. i m x
  2 1 3 _____

6. t l i f
  4 1 2 3 _____

7. m k i l
  1 4 2 3 _____

8. i h s t
  3 2 4 1 _____

9. f i
  2 1 _____

10. f g t i
  3 1 4 2 _____

11. h m i
  1 3 2 _____

12. i x s
  2 3 1 _____

13. s i m s
  3 2 1 4 _____

14. x f i
  3 1 2 _____

Get Word Wise
If you are a good painter, people will say you have a **gift** for painting.

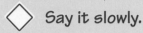
For Tomorrow

 See the word.

 Say it slowly.

☐ Link sounds and letters.

▽ Write.

⬡ Check.

Share What short i words did you find?

Spelling Words	
if	miss
gift	fix
lift	mix
him	six
milk	this

Spelling Words

up	duck
us	luck
bus	hunt
mud	bump
nut	put *LOOKOUT WORD*

Review	Challenge
this	puddle
came	puppy
run	

My Words

Words With Short u

A **See and Say**   b u s   d u ck
mu d   h u nt

These words have the short **u** sound. This vowel sound is spelled with the letter **u**.

B **Link Sounds and Letters**
Sort the spelling words. Write them on the lines.

See **us** in the bus.

Memory Jogger

_ u _
1. _____
2. _____
3. _____
4. _____

u _
5. _____
6. _____

_ u _ _
7. _____
8. _____
9. _____
10. _____

C **Write and Check**
Which words in the riddle have the short **u** sound?
Write the two spelling words.

11. _____   12. _____

Riddle
What is a duck when it jumps in the mud?
muddy

Ⓐ Rhyming Words
Say each picture name. Write the spelling word that rhymes.

1. _____

2. _____

3. _____

4. _____

5. _____

6. _____

Ⓑ Action Words
Write a word to finish the second sentence. Use a word in the first sentence.

7. A duck is flying over Sammy's head.
Quick, Sammy, ____!

_____

8. Jill has a big bump on her arm.
Try not to ____ it.

_____

9. The treasure hunt begins at 10 o'clock.
Then we will ____ for clues.

_____

Ⓒ Write
Write the spelling word that fits the word group.

_____

10. van, car, truck, _____

SPELL CHAT

Ask a friend to name a pair of short u words that rhyme.

Spelling Words	
up	duck
us	luck
bus	hunt
mud	bump
nut	put

Spelling Words

up	duck
us	luck
bus	hunt
mud	bump
nut	put

Review	Challenge
this	puddle
came	puppy
run	

My Words

_____

Quick Write

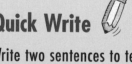

Write two sentences to tell what a trip to a farm might be like. Use one or more spelling words.

18   Lesson 3

You may do this activity on a computer.

A   Write Sentences

Picture yourself walking home from school in the rain. Write about what you could see. Use two or more spelling words.

_____

_____

_____

B   Proofread

Dustin wrote these sentences about his rainy walk home. He found two mistakes. Find four more mistakes that Dustin made, and fix them.

mud
Wet ⟨mudd⟩ is on everything. A duk is

swimming in the pond. i am op to my

knees in puddles. i will ron for cover.

Dustin

> **Tip**
> Always capitalize the word I. Remember: I am Important!

PROOFREADING MARKS

∧   Add
◯   Check spelling
—   Cross out
☰   Capital letter

Now proofread your sentences. Check your spelling. Be sure you wrote a capital **I** when writing about yourself.

Name . . . .

Ⓐ Use ABC Order
Write each set of letters in ABC order.

1. bedfc _____

2. truvs _____

3. kmonl _____

Ⓑ Test Yourself
Use the code to write the spelling words.

Ⓐ b ⬛ c 🔺 d ★ h 🔺 k ⬛ l ⬛ m ★ n 🔺 p ⬛ s ⚫ t ★ u

4. 🔺 ★ ⬛ _____

5. ★ ⬛ _____

6. 🔺 ★ ⚫ _____

7. ★ ★ ⚫ _____

8. ★ 🔺 _____

9. ⬛ ★ ⬛ 🔺 _____

10. ⚫ ★ ⚫ _____

11. ⚫ ★ ⬛ 🔺 _____

12. ★ ★ ⚫ _____

13. 🔺 ★ ⚫ 🔺 _____

Words With Short *u* 19

Get Word Wise
Some words sound like what they mean. **Bump** something. Do you hear **bump**?

For Tomorrow

➡️ See the word.

◇ Say it slowly.

⬜ Link sounds and letters.

▽ Write.

⬡ Check.

Share What short u words did you find?

Spelling Words	
up	duck
us	luck
bus	hunt
mud	bump
nut	put

Spelling Words

end
send
went
next
tell

well
help
mess
less
yes *LOOKOUT WORD*

Review	Challenge
put	lesson
nose	spend
let	

My Words

Words With Short e

A **See and Say**   s**e**nd   t**e**ll
n**e**xt   m**e**ss

These words have the short e sound.
This vowel sound is spelled with the letter e.

Y-E-S spells **yes**!

Memory Jogger

B **Link Sounds and Letters**
Sort the spelling words by the letters that come after **e**.
Write the words.

2 different letters

1. _____

2. _____

3. _____

4. _____

5. _____

1 letter

6. _____

2 alike letters

7. _____

8. _____

9. _____

10. _____

C **Write and Check**
What spelling word
answers the riddle?

11. _____

Riddle
What did the hen
say when she met
the elephant?

Ⓐ Word Meanings
Write a spelling word for each clue.

1. I'm not neat. I made a big _____.

2. You can't do it alone. You need my _____.

3. I'm not at the beginning. I'm at the _____.

4. You can get water from me. I'm a _____.

5. It's almost your turn. You're _____.

6. Don't say no! Say _____!

7. If you don't have more, you have _____.

Ⓑ Action Words
Write spelling words. The underlined words are clues.

8. I <u>sent</u> a letter last week. I'll _____ another today.

9. You <u>told</u> that story before. Please _____ it again.

10. We can <u>go</u> again even if we _____ there before.

SPELL CHAT

Tell a friend about the best thing you did today and the best thing you did yesterday. Use two or more spelling words.

Spelling Words	
end	well
send	help
went	mess
next	less
tell	yes

Name . . . .

Spelling Words

end	well
send	help
went	mess
next	less
tell	yes

Review	Challenge
put	lesson
nose	spend
let	

My Words

Quick Write

Think of a story about a family of birds. Write about something that happened to the baby bird. Use two or more spelling words.

A Write a Story
Write about a new pet you just got. Tell what the pet does and how you help care for it. Use two or more spelling words.

 You may do this activity on a computer.

B Proofread
Beth wrote this story about her pet. She found two mistakes. Find four more mistakes that Beth made, and fix them.

Tip
Start each sentence with a capital letter. Remember to write an ending mark.

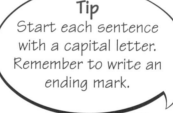

My new puppy is so funny. First he put
                           nose
his (nos) in his food. He made a big mes.

Nest he wend to sleep. At last he was

ready to play

Now proofread your story. Check your spelling.
Did you start each sentence with a capital letter?
Do all your sentences have ending marks?

Name . . . .

A Use ABC Order
Write each set of spelling words in ABC order.

send   next   tell   mess   yes   less

1. _____

2. _____

3. _____

4. _____

5. _____

6. _____

B Test Yourself
Write spelling words by filling in the missing letters.

7. y☐s

8. w☐☐

9. t☐☐☐

10. m☐☐☐

11. ☐☐n☐

12. ☐l☐

13. l☐☐☐

14. e☐☐

15. ☐☐☐t

16. ☐☐☐l

Get Word Wise
Long ago, a **mess** was a group of people who ate together. Their table manners must have been a **mess**.

For Tomorrow

→ See the word.

◇ Say it slowly.

☐ Link sounds and letters.

▽ Write.

⬡ Check.

Share What short e words did you find?

Spelling Words

end	well
send	help
went	mess
next	less
tell	yes

LESSON 5

Spelling Words

on	rock
odd	socks
lot	box
spot	fox
stop	off LOOKOUT WORD

Review	Challenge
yes	rocket
meet	spotted
not	

My Words

Words With Short o

A **See and Say**   on   lot
odd   rock

These words have the short o sound.
This vowel sound is spelled with the letter o.

> **Socks** has five letters—one for each toe on a foot.
>
> Memory Jogger

B **Link Sounds and Letters**

Sort the spelling words. Write them on the lines.

o _

1. _____

o _ _

2. _____

3. _____

_ o _

4. _____

5. _____

6. _____

_ o _ _

7. _____

_ _ o _

8. _____

9. _____

_ o _ _ _

10. _____

C **Write and Check**

What two things make the odd fox different?
Both are spelling words. Write them here.

11. _____   12. _____

Vocabulary Practice

Name . . . .

Ⓐ Opposites
Write the opposite of each word. Use a spelling word.

1. on _____

2. even _____

3. go _____

4. off _____

Ⓑ Plurals
Write the spelling word that tells about more than one. Use the picture clue.

5. _____

Add **s** to spelling words to tell about each picture.

6. _____

7. _____

Add **es** to spelling words that end in **x**.

8. _____

9. _____

Ⓒ Write
Write a sentence with **lot** and one of these words. **rock box spot fox**

10. _____

Be a Spelling Sleuth
Look at labels for two words with the short o sound, such as **spot** and **rock**.

SPELL CHAT

Work with a friend. Name another pair of opposites. One word should have the short o sound.

Spelling Words	
on	rock
odd	socks
lot	box
spot	fox
stop	off

Spelling Words

on	rock
odd	socks
lot	box
spot	fox
stop	off

Review	Challenge
yes	rocket
meet	spotted
not	

My Words

Quick Write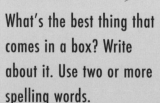

What's the best thing that comes in a box? Write about it. Use two or more spelling words.

A **Write in a**

A surprise gift has come in the mail. What will you write in your 📓? Write it below. Use two or more spelling words.

You may do this activity on a computer.

B **Proofread**

Tom wrote this in his . He found two mistakes. Find four more mistakes that Tom made, and fix them.

Tip
Remember to write an ending mark for each sentence.

Monday, September 30

Today I got a big ⟨boks⟩ from Uncle Bob.
　　　　　　　box

Yess I did! He sent me a rok with od

spots on it, Wait until after dinner

Then I will write more.　　Tom

PROOFREADING MARKS
∧ Add
◯ Check spelling
— Cross out
≡ Capital letter

Now proofread what you wrote. Check your spelling. Be sure every sentence has an ending mark.

Study and Review

Name ....

Ⓐ Use ABC Order
Write each set of spelling words in ABC order.

lot	fox	box

1. _____

2. _____

3. _____

rock	odd	stop

4. _____

5. _____

6. _____

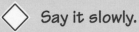

Ⓑ Test Yourself
Write spelling words by filling in the missing letters.

7. s⬜⬜⬜

8. l⬜

9. r⬜⬜

10. s⬜⬜

11. ⬜⬜⬜

12. ⬜f

13. ⬜d

14. b⬜⬜

15. o⬜

16. ⬜⬜

Spelling Words	
on	rock
odd	socks
lot	box
spot	fox
stop	off

Name . . . .

Problems at the Pond

Write a spelling word to finish each sentence.
Then use the word that's left to answer the question.

ask   help   if   up   yes   off

Freddy Frog wants to pick __(1)__ the rocks.

He wants to get them __(2)__ the beach.

He will __(3)__ Fanny to help him. Fanny has a

big family. __(4)__ they all __(5)__, will the job get

done? __(6)__

box   rock   stop   six

Fanny Frog has ten rocks. She drops one __(7)__

in a puddle. She leaves two at the bus __(8)__. She

meets Freddy and gives him one. She puts the rest in

a __(9)__. How many rocks does Fanny put in the

box? __(10)__

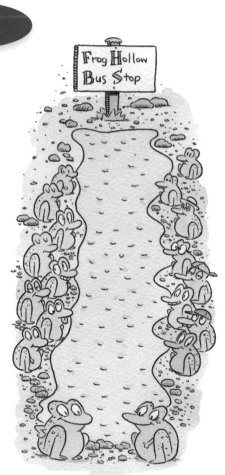

Frog Hollow Bus Stop

1. _____

2. _____

3. _____

4. _____

5. _____

6. _____

7. _____

8. _____

9. _____

10. _____

Rhyme Time

Write a spelling word to finish each rhyme.

mad

lot

bump

1. This dog has one spot.

_____

That dog has a _____!

2. Hop, skip. Hop, jump.

_____

Hop, trip. Hop, _____.

3. I feel so glad,

_____

I can't be _____.

What Do You Hear?.........................

Read each group of words. Listen for the vowel sound. Write the spelling word that fits.

us   ask   miss   well   socks

4. am   hand   add   _____

5. gift   milk   fix   _____

6. nut   up   hunt   _____

7. send   next   less   _____

8. spot   rock   fox   _____

Write Here ....

Mix up the letters in the word **post**. Write two spelling words.

9. _____

10. _____

Lesson 6 Review

What Would You Say?
What if these things happened to you? Write what you would say. Use one or two spelling words each time.

Spelling words:
ask   mud
has   put
was   went
mad   tell
him   help
miss   lot

1. You lost your homework.

2. You know a secret about Dad.

3. You have a big job to do.

4. You ate the last apple.

Look at the words you spelled wrong on your Unit 1 Post-Tests. Use some of them to write what these children could be saying.

5.

What's Next?
Write what the children might say the next time.

6.

Tip
Remember to write the word **I** with a capital letter.

Proofread your sentences. Make sure your spelling, capitalization, and end marks are correct.

PROOFREADING MARKS
∧ Add
○ Check spelling
— Cross out
≡ Capital letter

Write the Correct Word

Read each sentence. Circle the word with the wrong letter. Write the correct word on the line.

1. Let me tall you a secret. _____

2. Carol his a birthday next week. _____

3. Gus want to the store. _____

4. He wax going to buy a gift. _____

5. Who went with hem? _____

6. Sam pat a toy in the box. _____

7. The box fell in the mad. _____

8. Keesha is not feeling will. _____

9. I hope she won't mess the party. _____

Ray Says...

Don't use the wrong letter in a word. I wrote "Don't be **mud**." But I should have written "Don't be **mad**." My friend was really mad then!

well

was

mud

miss

went

has

put

tell

him

Spelling Matters!

Spelling Words

come	none
some	love
from	of
one	gone
done	does

LOOKOUT WORDS

Review	Challenge
off	once
clean	above
home	

My Words

Name ....

More Words With Short u

Think **of** this:
off - f = **of**
Of course!

Ⓐ **See and Say**   come   from
done   of

In these words, the short u sound is spelled o.

Memory Jogger

Ⓑ **Link Sounds and Letters**
Sort the spelling words. Write them on the lines.

o-consonant-e

1. _____   3. _____   6. _____

2. _____   4. _____   7. _____

5. _____

o

8. _____   9. _____   10. _____

Ⓒ **Write and Check**
Which words in the poem have the short **u** sound?
Write the three spelling words.

_____

11. _____

Poem
"Yum"
Baked bun.
Ate one.
Now none.
Story done!

Name ....

A Riddle Rhymes

Write a spelling word to answer each riddle. _____

1. It starts like  and rhymes with **of**.

2. It starts like and rhymes with **fun**.

3. It starts like and rhymes with **gum**.

4. It starts like and rhymes with **glove**.

5. It sounds just like **sum**.

6. It sounds just like **won**.

B Action Words

Write a word to finish each sentence.
Use a spelling word from the box.

gone   come   done   does

7. Fall has _____ again.

8. Mia has _____ her work and has _____ to sleep.

9. Who _____ this book belong to?

Spelling Words	
come	none
some	love
from	of
one	gone
done	does

Spelling Words

come	none
some	love
from	of
one	gone
done	does

Review	Challenge
off	once
clean	above
home	

My Words

Quick Write

What does your family like to do together? Write about it. Use a spelling word.

Name ....

You may do this activity on a computer.

A Write a Poem

Use spelling words to finish this poem about a special family time. Try to make the poem rhyme.

_____

Dinner is ready, the food is _____.

_____

So _____ to the table, everyone!

B Proofread

Monisha wrote this poem. She found two mistakes. Find four more mistakes that Monisha made, and fix them.

Tip
People's names are special. They always begin with capital letters.

It's Grandma addie's birthday.

She's 61. Let's have a party for

Grandma addie! Let's have ~~soem~~ *some* fun!

No matter where you're coming frum.

Don't put it of ! Everybody com !

Monisha

PROOFREADING MARKS

∧ Add
◯ Check spelling
— Cross out
≡ Capital letter

Now proofread the poem you finished. Did you spell the words correctly?

Study and Review

Name ....

A Use ABC Order
Write each set of spelling words in ABC order.

love none gone

1. _____ 2. _____ 3. _____

does from come

4. _____ 5. _____ 6. _____

B Test Yourself
What are the missing letters? Write the whole spelling word.

7. ☐ v ☐

8. ☐ f

9. ☐ ☐ s

10. ☐ r ☐ ☐

11. n ☐ ☐ ☐

12. g ☐ ☐

13. c ☐ ☐ ☐

14. ☐ n ☐

15. d ☐ ☐ e

16. s ☐ ☐ ☐

Get Word Wise
Combine **some** and **one**. It's **someone**! What other words can you make with **some**?

For Tomorrow

 See the word.

 Say it slowly.

 Link sounds and letters.

 Write.

Check.

Share What short u words spelled with o did you find?

Spelling Words	
come	none
some	love
from	of
one	gone
done	does

Spelling Words

than	think
that	bath
them	both
then	with
these	there

There tells where.

Memory Jogger

Review	Challenge
gone	mother
has	father
those	

My Words

Words With th

A **See and Say**

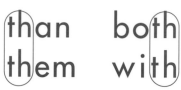

than   both
them   with

The letters th together stand for the first sound you hear in **than**.

B **Link Sounds and Letters**
Sort the spelling words. Write them on the lines.

Words That Start With th

1. _____   3. _____   6. _____

2. _____   4. _____   7. _____

5. _____

Words That End With th

8. _____   9. _____   10. _____

C **Write and Check**
Write the spelling word that finishes the answer to the riddle.

_____

11. the _____ water

Riddle
What goes up when you get in and down when you get out?

Name ....

A Sentence Clues
Write **then** or **than** to finish each sentence.

1. My dog likes a bath better _____ I do.

2. Ruffy gets out, _____ he shakes.

3. I'm wetter _____ Ruffy!

B Make New Words
Change the underlined letter in each word to write a spelling word.

4. th<u>e</u>m _____

5. tha<u>n</u> _____

6. the<u>n</u> _____

7. wi<u>s</u>h _____

8. <u>p</u>ath _____

9. th<u>a</u>nk _____

10. th<u>e</u>n _____

11. <u>m</u>oth _____

12. the<u>r</u>e _____

13. the<u>s</u>e _____

Be a Spelling Sleuth
Look on cereal boxes for two words that start or end with the letters th, such as **this** or **with**.

SPELL CHAT

With a partner, make up a sentence using **than**. Make up another sentence using **then**.

Spelling Words	
than	think
that	bath
them	both
then	with
these	there

Name

Spelling Words

than	think
that	bath
them	both
then	with
these	there

Review	Challenge
gone	mother
has	father
those	

My Words

Quick Write

Write how two story characters are alike and how they are different. Use two or more spelling words.

A Write About a Picture

Draw a picture from your favourite folk tale. Then write one or two sentences about the picture. Use at least two spelling words.

You may do this activity on a computer.

B Proofread

Nick wrote these sentences about his picture. He found two mistakes. Find four more mistakes that Nick made, and fix them.

Tip
It's easy to make a mistake with some words. Be sure to use **then** and **than** correctly. Also watch out for **there** and **their**!

has
The troll (haz) tried and tried to

stop thees goats.

He does not want tham

to go over their

Now proofread your sentences. Check your spelling. Be sure you put the correct mark at the end of each sentence.

PROOFREADING MARKS

∧ Add
◯ Check spelling
— Cross out
≡ Capital letter

Name . . . .

Ⓐ Use ABC Order

Put a check in the box if the words are in ABC order.
If not, write the words in ABC order.

1. ☐ gone   bath   that   3. ☐ both   goat   them

2. ☐ some   think   with   4. ☐ these   rock   has

_____

- -

_____

Ⓑ Test Yourself

Write a spelling word for each clue.

5. not here   _____

6. not now   _____

7. not a shower, but a   _____

8. not one   _____

9. not without   _____

10. not us   _____

11. not this   _____

12. not those   _____

13. taller ____ me   _____

14. I ____ so!   _____

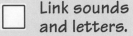

Get Word Wise

Long ago, th was one letter. It was called **thorn**, and it looked like this:

For Tomorrow

 See the word.

◇ Say it slowly.

☐ Link sounds and letters.

▽ Write.

⬤ Check.

Share What th words did you find?

Spelling Words	
than	think
that	bath
them	both
then	with
these	there

Spelling Words

shell   dish

ship   fish

shop   wish

sheep   rush

shut   push

LOOKOUT WORD

Review	Challenge
there	shape
miss	finish
she	

My Words

Words With sh

A   **See and Say**   shell   wish
                       sheep   push

The letters **sh** together stand for the first sound you hear in **shell**.

"Shhh," says the **sheep**.

B **Link Sounds and Letters**

Sort the spelling words. Write them on the lines.

Words That Start With sh

1. _____
2. _____
3. _____
4. _____
5. _____

Words That End With sh

6. _____
7. _____
8. _____
9. _____
10. _____

C **Write and Check**

Read the button. Write the two spelling words.

11. _____
12. _____

Say this five times fast! Shall she sell the shell shop?

Name . . . .

A Famous Sayings
Write a spelling word to finish each saying.

1. counting _____

2. _____ on a star

B Make New Words
Change the underlined letter to **sh**. Then write the spelling word you make.

3. pu<u>t</u> _____

4. <u>h</u>op _____

5. di<u>p</u> _____

6. <u>k</u>eep _____

7. ru<u>n</u> _____

8. <u>b</u>ut _____

9. wi<u>n</u> _____

10. <u>d</u>ip _____

11. fi<u>t</u> _____

12. <u>t</u>ell _____

Be a Spelling Sleuth
Look on posters for at least two words with sh, as in **shell** and **push**.

SPELL CHAT

With the person sitting next to you, make up a saying using sh words. Use two or more spelling words.

Spelling Words	
shell	dish
ship	fish
shop	wish
sheep	rush
shut	push

Spelling Words

shell	dish
ship	fish
shop	wish
sheep	rush
shut	push

Review	Challenge
there	shape
miss	finish
she	

My Words

Quick Write

Write one sentence telling which would make a better pet: a sheep or a fish. Use two spelling words.

A Write a Funny Story

Write a short story about something that happens every day. Make your story funny. Use two or more spelling words.

You may do this activity on a computer.

B Proofread

Ed wrote a funny story. He found two mistakes. Find four more mistakes that Ed made, and fix them.

> There
> ⊙Ther⊙ is the shop that had the ˄dish.
>   biggest
>
> My dsh was than the other.
>
> I wanted to puch it out the door,
>
> but the door was sut !

Tip

Add **-er** to a describing word to compare two people or things. Add **-est** to compare more than two.

PROOFREADING MARKS

∧ Add
◯ Check spelling
— Cross out
≡ Capital letter

Now proofread your story. Check your spelling. Did you add **-er** and **-est** to words that compare?

Name..

A Use ABC Order

Write these words in ABC order. | there   push   wish   rush   shop |

1. _____

2. _____

3. _____

4. _____

5. _____

B Test Yourself

Write a spelling word that rhymes with each word.
Some have more than one answer.
Use each spelling word only once.

6. yell _____

7. tip _____

8. fish _____

9. sleep _____

10. dish _____

11. crush _____

12. bush _____

13. wish _____

14. pop _____

15. but _____

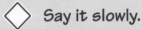

Get Word Wise

The word **sheep** can name one sheep or a whole group of sheep.

For Tomorrow

 See the word.

◇ Say it slowly.

☐ Link sounds and letters.

▽ Write.

⬡ Check.

Share What sh words did you find?

Spelling Words	
shell	dish
ship	fish
shop	wish
sheep	rush
shut	push

Spelling Words

chip	such
chop	bunch
rich	lunch
which	branch
much	ache

LOOKOUT WORD

Review	Challenge
push	children
bump	stomach
hop	

My Words

Words With ch

Ⓐ **See and Say**   ch ip   whi ch
ch op   lun ch

The letters ch together stand for the first sound you hear in **chip**.

Ⓑ **Link Sounds and Letters**
Sort the spelling words. Write the words on the lines.

Start With ch

1. _____

2. _____

End With ich

3. _____

4. _____

End With nch

5. _____

6. _____

7. _____

End With uch

8. _____

9. _____

_ch_

10. _____

Ⓒ **Write and Check**
Read the button. Write the three spelling words.

11. _____

Remember this!
Too mu**ch** cake
Will make you a**ch**e.

Memory Jogger

Say this five times fast!
How much lunch can a bunch munch ?

A   Word Puzzles

Solve each word puzzle to make a spelling word.
Write the spelling word on the line.

1. sun - n + ch = _____

2. ch - h + hop = _____

3. ch - h + hip = _____

4. act - t + he = _____

5. rip - p + ch = _____

6. bunk - k + ch = _____

7. lung - g + ch = _____

8. whip - p + ch = _____

9. mud - d + ch = _____

10. brand - d + ch = _____

B   More Than One

Add **-es** to words that end with **ch** to name
more than one.
Add **-es** to a spelling word to tell about
each picture.

  11. _____

 12. _____

 13. _____

 14. _____

Be a Spelling Sleuth

Look on school signs for two words with ch, as in **chop** or **lunch**.

SPELL CHAT

With a friend, make up a word puzzle for **chair** and another one for **child**.

Spelling Words	
chip	such
chop	bunch
rich	lunch
which	branch
much	ache

Name . . . .

Spelling Words

chip	such
chop	bunch
rich	lunch
which	branch
much	ache

Review	Challenge
push	children
bump	stomach
hop	

My Words

Quick Write ✏️

Think about your favourite story. Write what you like best about it. Use one or more spelling words.

A **Write What Story Characters Say**

Imagine that two of your favourite story characters meet. Write what they say to each other. Use two or more spelling words.

 You may do this activity on a computer.

B **Proofread**

Carlos wrote what two characters said. He found two mistakes. Find four more mistakes and fix them.

"Stop!" said the Troll. "I will eat you for lunch

(luch)!" "You don't scare me very mush,"

said the Wolf. "I'll use a brach

to posh you off this bridge!

Tip

Remember to put a quotation mark before the first word and after the last word that someone says.

PROOFREADING MARKS

∧ Add
◯ Check spelling
— Cross out
≡ Capital letter

Now proofread your own sentences. Check your spelling. Did you put quotation marks around the words characters say?

Ⓐ Use ABC Order

Write each set of words in ABC order.

| push   much   lunch |

1. _____   2. _____   3. _____

| such   rich   which |

4. _____   5. _____   6. _____

Ⓑ Test Yourself

Fill in the missing letters to write a spelling word. Then use the boxed letters to write two more spelling words.

7. a □ _____

8. w _____ □

9. r □ _____

10. _____ o □

11. _____

12. □ _____ a _____

13. m □ _____

14. l □ _____

15. s □ □

16. _____

Get Word Wise

If you act like one of your parents, someone might say you're a "**chip** off the old block!"

For Tomorrow

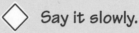 See the word.

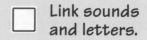 Say it slowly.

 Link sounds and letters.

 Write.

Check.

Share What ch words did you find?

Spelling Words	
chip	such
chop	bunch
rich	lunch
which	branch
much	ache

Spelling Words

stand	last
stamp	best
stick	rest
stone	must
fast	taste

LOOKOUT WORD

Review	Challenge
ache	listen
next	student
still	

My Words

Words With st

A **See and Say**   stand   best
stone   must

The letters st stand for the first sounds you hear in **stone** and the last sounds in **best**.

B **Link Sounds and Letters**
Say the spelling words. Write them on the lines.

Start With st

1. _____
2. _____
3. _____
4. _____

End With st

5. _____
6. _____
7. _____
8. _____
9. _____
10. _____

C **Write and Check**
Write the four spelling words in the poem.

11. _____

Don't forget the la**st** letters in **last**!

Memory Jogger

Poem
The best
finish fast.
The rest
follow last.

Ⓐ Opposites

Write a spelling word that is the opposite of each word.

1. slow _____

2. sit _____

3. first _____

Ⓑ Make New Words

Change the underlined letter in each word to **st**.
Write the spelling word.

4. mu<u>d</u> _____

5. <u>c</u>amp _____

6. re<u>d</u> _____

7. <u>b</u>one _____

8. la<u>p</u> _____

9. ta<u>k</u>e _____

10. be<u>d</u> _____

11. fa<u>n</u> _____

12. <u>k</u>ick _____

13. <u>h</u>and _____

Words With *st* (49)

Be a Spelling Sleuth

Look on street signs for at least two words with the letters st, such as **stop**.

SPELL CHAT

With a partner, think of a pair of opposites. Use one of the spelling words in the pair.

Spelling Words	
stand	last
stamp	best
stick	rest
stone	must
fast	taste

Spelling Words

stand	last
stamp	best
stick	rest
stone	must
fast	taste

Review	Challenge
ache	listen
next	student
still	

My Words

Quick Write

Think about messages on posters and signs. Write your own message. Use two spelling words.

A Write a Sign

Make a sign with a message on it. Tell others about a new club or a book you read. Use naming words and two or more spelling words.

 You may do this activity on a computer.

B Proofread

Stacey wrote a sign about the stamp club. She found two mistakes. Find four more mistakes that Stacey made, and fix them.

> **Tip**
> Naming words name people, places, and things.

STAMP CLUB
    stamp club
The ⟨samp⟩∧ will meet nxt Friday

at Stacey's house. You mus bring

your bess stamps. Call for how

to get to her house.   Stacey

PROOFREADING MARKS
∧ Add
◯ Check spelling
— Cross out
≡ Capital letter

Now proofread your sign. Check the spelling. Be sure to include naming words.

A Use ABC Order
Write each set of words in ABC order.

| next |
| lunch |
| must |
| last |

1. _____

2. _____

3. _____

4. _____

| stamp |
| such |
| sheep |
| some |

5. _____

6. _____

7. _____

8. _____

B Test Yourself
Write spelling words by filling in the missing letters.

9.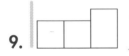

10.

11.

12.

13.

14.

15.

16.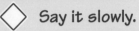

17.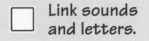

18.

Get Word Wise
Fast can mean "quickly." But it can also mean "to go without food."

For Tomorrow
➡ See the word.

◇ Say it slowly.

▢ Link sounds and letters.

▽ Write.

⬡ Check.

Share What st words did you find?

Spelling Words

stand	last
stamp	best
stick	rest
stone	must
fast	taste

Name...

A Tale of Two Sheep

Write a spelling word to finish each sentence.

sheep   wish   think   with

One day, two sheep were talking. "I'm tired of staying __(1)__ the dog," said the first __(2)__ . "I __(3)__ we could go someplace without him."

"I __(4)__ we should," said the other sheep. And so they did.

shop   gone   stand   taste   fast   lunch

The two sheep had not __(5)__ far when they saw a __(6)__ . "Don't just __(7)__ there," Mr. Wolf the shopkeeper said. "Come in, and __(8)__ the food."

Just then the dog rushed in. He pushed the wolf and said to the sheep, "Get out __(9)__ . Don't have lunch here, unless you want to be __(10)__ !"

1. _____
2. _____
3. _____
4. _____
5. _____
6. _____
7. _____
8. _____
9. _____
10. _____

Make It Rhyme

Write a spelling word to finish each sentence.
The spelling word rhymes with the underlined words.

1. _____ <u>cat</u> is <u>fat</u>!

2. <u>Please</u> <u>freeze</u> _____ <u>peas</u>.

3. This <u>cake</u> will <u>make</u> <u>Jake</u> _____ .

4. _____ way will <u>Mitch</u> <u>pitch</u>?

these
which
that
ache

Opposites . . . .

Come and **go** are opposites. **Hot** and **cold** are too.
Write the spelling word that is the opposite of each word.

5. pull _____

6. to _____

7. open _____

8. poor _____

shut
from
push
rich

Mix-Up! . . . .

Change one letter in each word to make a spelling word.

9. such _____

10. where _____

there
much

Name . . . .

come   shop
from   sheep
gone   push
does   much
these   fast
with   must

Another Sheep Tale

Answer these questions to help plan your own sheep story. Use spelling words to write your ideas.

Tip
Remember to begin each sentence with a capital letter. End each sentence with the correct mark.

What is the story about?
_____
- -
1. _____

What is the problem?
_____
- -
2. _____

What must the sheep do?
_____
- -
3. _____

Look at the words you spelled wrong on your Unit 2 Post-Tests. Use some of them to write more ideas for your story.

_____
- -
4. _____
_____

Give It a Title . . . .

Write a title for your story.

_____
- -
5. _____

Proofread your title for spelling and capitalization. Then make a book cover using that title.

PROOFREADING MARKS
. . . .
∧   Add
◯   Check spelling
—   Cross out
≡   Capital letter

Name . . . .

Rhyming Words

Write the spelling word that rhymes with the words in each list.

must
best
come
does

buzz   was   fuzz

1. _____

dressed   guessed   nest

3. _____

dust   fussed   just

2. _____

hum   some   from

4. _____

Spelling Matters!

these
one
there
ache

bear   care   fair

5. _____

bake   make   wake

7. _____

bees   please   trees

6. _____

fun   run   sun

8. _____

Spelling Words

name	place
same	snake
save	wake
brave	skate
face	*have* LOOKOUT WORD

Review	Challenge
taste	blame
stop	chase
make	

My Words

_____

_____

_____

_____

_____

Words With Long a

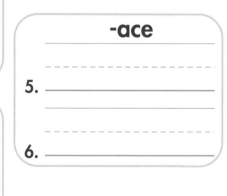

*I "c" my **face** in the mirror.*

A   See and Say    name   face
save   snake

These words have the long a sound. This sound is spelled a-consonant-e.

B Link Sounds and Letters

Sort the spelling words. Write them on the lines.

-ake

1. _____

2. _____

-ame

3. _____

4. _____

-ace

5. _____

6. _____

-ave

7. _____

8. _____

9. _____

-ate

10. _____

C Write and Check

Write a spelling word to answer the riddle.

_____

11. your _____

Riddle
What is yours, but is used more by others?

Vocabulary Practice

Name ....

Ⓐ Make New Words

Change one letter in each word to make a spelling word. Write the word on the line.

1. lake _____

2. lace _____

3. slate _____

4. shake _____

5. brake _____

6. tame _____

7. hive _____

8. gave _____

9. sale _____

10. plate _____

Ⓑ Add -ing

Take off the **e** at the end of the word. Then add **-ing.** Write the new words.

skate + ing = skating

11. save _____

12. wake _____

13. have _____

Be a Spelling Sleuth

Look in school messages for three words with the long a sound spelled a-consonant-e, such as **name**.

SPELL CHAT

Talk with a friend. Name two things you can do that have the long a sound. Use at least one spelling word.

Spelling Words	
name	place
same	snake
save	wake
brave	skate
face	have

Spelling Words

name	place
same	snake
save	wake
brave	skate
face	have

Review	Challenge
taste	blame
stop	chase
make	

My Words

Quick Write

Think about when you were **brave**. What happened? Use two or more spelling words to write about it.

A Write a Folk Tale

Think about folk tales. What are the characters like? What happens to them? Write the start of a folk tale. Use two or more spelling words.

» You may do this activity on a computer.

B Proofread

Erin wrote this folk tale about a snake. She found two mistakes. Find four more mistakes that Erin made, and fix them.

Spelling Tip
When you add **-ing** to a word that ends in **e**, remember to take off the **e**. Then add **-ing**.

brave
Once there was a ~~bray~~ snaik . His
waking
nam was Jake. When he was ~~wakeing~~
up, he saw a fox skateing off with
a hen. Jake hurried to say the hen.
Erin

PROOFREADING MARKS
∧ Add
◯ Check spelling
— Cross out
≡ Capital letter

Now proofread your folk tale. Check your spelling. Make sure each sentence has a naming part and a doing part.

Name ....

Ⓐ Use the Dictionary: **Guide Words**

Guide words are at the top of a dictionary page.
They tell the first and last words on the page.

> **waiting room** ► **walrus**
>
> **waiting room** noun A room or an area where people sit and wait for something such as a train, an airplane, or a doctor's appointment.
>
> 2. Anything that blocks the way, shuts something in, or divides one thing from another; a barrier, as in *a wall of marchers, wall of fire, wall of secrecy.*

Circle the guide words on the dictionary page.
Which words could you find on this page?

why   walk   wake

1. _____   2. _____

Ⓑ Test Yourself

Write spelling words by filling in the missing letters.

3. b☐☐☐☐

4. ☐v☐

5. ☐k☐☐

6. ☐a☐

7. n☐☐☐

8. ☐l☐☐☐

9. s☐☐☐

10. ☐☐m☐

11. ☐☐v☐

12. ☐☐☐e

Get Word Wise

Snakes are often feared. So the word **snake** may mean "a person not to be trusted."

For Tomorrow

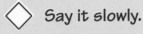 See the word.

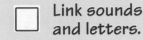 Say it slowly.

 Link sounds and letters.

 Write.

 Check.

Share What long a words did you find?

Spelling Words

name	place
same	snake
save	wake
brave	skate
face	have

Spelling Words

away	mail
may	rain
pay	paint
play	afraid
today	said

LOOKOUT WORD

Review	Challenge
have	snail
does	playmate
may	

My Words

Learn and Spell

Name ....

More Words With Long a

You say. I said.

Memory Jogger

A **See and Say**   may   rain
play   paint

These words have the long a sound. The sound is spelled with the letters ay or ai.

B **Link Sounds and Letters**

Sort the spelling words. Write them on the lines.

Words That End With ay

1. _____   3. _____   5. _____

2. _____   4. _____

Words With ai in the Middle

6. _____   8. _____   10. _____

7. _____   9. _____

C **Write and Check**

Read the riddle. Write the spelling word with the long a sound. Circle the letters that stand for the sound.

11. _____

Riddle
What did the dirt say to the rain?
You make me mud!

Vocabulary Practice

Name . . . .

Ⓐ Use Clues

Write one or two spelling words to finish each sentence.

_____

1. Put the _____ in the box.

2. Let's _____ ball!

3. The _____ wet my hat.

4. Sam _____ he is _____.

5. I'll _____ for lunch _____.

Ⓑ Words That Tell Where or When

Write a spelling word to finish each sentence. The word should tell where or when.

_____

6. Mom said I can play _____.

_____

7. I wish the rain would go _____.

Be a Spelling Sleuth

Look at some mail for words with the long a sound spelled **ay** or **ai**. Find three words.

SPELL CHAT

With a friend, pick a spelling word. Use the word in two ways, such as:
I **mail** the letter.
I got **mail** today.

Spelling Words	
away	mail
may	rain
pay	paint
play	afraid
today	said

Spelling Words

away	mail
may	rain
pay	paint
play	afraid
today	said

Review	Challenge
have	snail
does	playmate
may	

My Words

Quick Write

Write two sentences to tell about a rainy day. Use two or more spelling words.

 You may do this activity on a computer.

Ⓐ Write About a Picture

Draw a picture of something fun you did yesterday. Write about it. Use spelling words.

Ⓑ Proofread

Suni wrote this about her picture. She found two mistakes. Find four more mistakes that Suni made, and fix them.

Tip
Remember that **I** is used in the naming part of a sentence. **Me** is used in the telling part.

```
              does
The sky (duz) look cloudy. My
              I
sister and me are not afrad. We

pla in the rayn. Then my sister

and me go in the house.

                    Suni
```

PROOFREADING MARKS

∧ Add
◯ Check spelling
— Cross out
≡ Capital letter

Proofread what you wrote. Check your spelling. Make sure you used **I** and **me** correctly.

Ⓐ Use the Dictionary: **The Entry**

A dictionary has an entry for each word. An entry gives information about a word.

part of speech

entry word

the meaning of the word

rain *noun* Water falling in the form of drops from clouds. *I like to play in the rain.*
▷ *verb* **rain** *It rained all day.*

example sentence

part of speech

example sentence

Write a sentence about rain.

1. _____

Ⓑ Test Yourself

Use the code to write the spelling words.

a **d** **f** **g** **p** **l** **m** **n** **o** **p** **r** **s** **t** **w** **y**

2. ★◆♠★ _____

3. ◆♠ _____

4. ◆♠ _____

5. ◆♠ _____

6. ◆♠ _____

7. ◆◆♠ _____

8. ◆♠⬤ _____

9. ⬤★◆♠ _____

10. ◆⬤◆◆♠★ _____

11. ◆♥◆♠ _____

Get Word Wise

Have you ever watched a possum? When you "**play** possum," you pretend to be asleep.

For Tomorrow

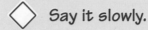 See the word.

◇ Say it slowly.

☐ Link sounds and letters.

▽ Write.

⬤ Check.

Share What long *a* words did you find?

Spelling Words	
away	mail
may	rain
pay	paint
play	afraid
today	said

MAIN ST.

CHAPEL ST.

Learn and Spell

Name . . . .

Words With Long e

A **See and Say** three beat

need each

These words have the long e sound. The sound is spelled ee or ea.

Isn't it funny? Three has two e's.

Memory Jogger

B **Link Sounds and Letters**

Sort the spelling words. Write them on the lines.

Spelling Words

three	beat
agree	easy
feel	each
need	dream
street	great

LOOKOUT WORD

Review	Challenge
said	cheetah
these	creature
green	

My Words

ee

1. _____

2. _____

3. _____

4. _____

5. _____

ea

6. _____

7. _____

8. _____

9. _____

10. _____

Vocabulary Practice

Name ....

A Use Clues
Use the clue to write a spelling word.

1. The number between 2 and 4 is _____.

2. You could live on the main _____.

3. Sometimes you _____ when you sleep.

4. You _____ when you say yes.

5. If you _____ the clock, you win.

6. If something is not hard, it's _____.

7. It wasn't a bad day, but a _____ day!

8. If you called _____ day, you called every day.

B Action Words
Write the spelling word that tells about now.

Past	needed	Past	felt
Now	9. _____	Now	10. _____

Be a Spelling Sleuth
Look in ads for three words with the long e sound, such as **feet** and **seat**.

SPELL CHAT

Tell a friend how you feel today. Ask how your friend felt yesterday. Use one or more spelling words.

Spelling Words	
three	beat
agree	easy
feel	each
need	dream
street	great

Spelling Words

three	beat
agree	easy
feel	each
need	dream
street	great

Review	Challenge
said	cheetah
these	creature
green	

My Words

Quick Write

Think about when you had a great time doing something. Write three sentences about it. Use two or more spelling words.

Ⓐ Write About a Book

Think of a book you read and liked. Write a few sentences telling your classmates why they should read it. Use two or more spelling words.

You may do this activity on a computer.

Ⓑ Proofread

Timmy wrote about a favourite book. He found two mistakes. Find three more mistakes that Timmy made, and fix them.

Tip
The name of a special place or person always begins with a capital letter.

To My Class,
⎯⎯⎯⎯⎯ need
You ⟨ned⟩ to read The Funny Frog. It's

about a grene frog and a boy named

≡luis who lives in Toronto. It's a grayt

book! It is esy to read.

Timmy

PROOFREADING MARKS

∧ Add
◯ Check spelling
— Cross out
≡ Capital letter

Proofread your sentences. Check your spelling. Be sure you used capital letters where they are needed.

Ⓐ Use the Dictionary: **Definition**

A definition tells the meaning of a word. Read the entry and find the definition.

Write the spelling word that goes with each definition.

> **three**
>
> 1. *noun* The whole number, written 3, that comes after 2 and before 4.

1. A road in a city or town _____

2. To say yes to something _____

Ⓑ Test Yourself

Write spelling words by filling in **ea** or **ee**.

3. b___ ___ t

4. n___ ___ d

5. ___ ___ ch

6. f ___ ___ l

7. ___ ___ sy

8. dr ___ ___ m

9. thr ___ ___

10. gr ___ ___ t

11. str ___ ___ t

12. agr ___ ___

Get Word Wise

Street comes from an old word that means "to stretch out."

For Tomorrow

 See the word.

 Say it slowly.

 Link sounds and letters.

 Write.

◉ Check.

Share What long e words did you find?

Spelling Words	
three	beat
agree	easy
feel	each
need	dream
street	great

Name ....

Words That End With y

A **See and Say** | many | happy
story | pretty

These words end with the long e sound. The sound
is spelled with the letter y.

See **ever**
in **every**.

Memory Jogger

Spelling Words

any	pretty
many	funny
very	sorry
every	story
happy	money

Review	Challenge
great	fantasy
shop	mystery
my	

My Words

LOOKOUT
WORD

B **Link Sounds and Letters**

Sort the spelling words. Write them on the lines.

One Consonant Before y

1. _____ 5. _____

2. _____

3. _____

4. _____

Vowel Before y

6. _____

Double Consonant Before y

7. _____

8. _____

9. _____

10. _____

C **Write and Check**

Write two spelling words to tell about the picture.

11. _____   12. _____

Name . . . .

Be a Spelling Sleuth

Look in a store sign for three words that end in y, such as **happy**.

A **Sentence Clues**
Write a spelling word to answer each riddle.

1. You can find me in a book. What am I? _____

2. Look for me in the bank. What am I? _____

3. I rhyme with Jerry, but I'm not a name. What am I? _____

B **Describing Words**
A describing word tells how something looks, sounds, or feels.
It can tell how many. Write spelling words that describe.

4. I don't have _____ money.

5. I am _____ about the mess.

6. How _____ shells do you have?

7. Do you eat some fruit _____ day?

8. I feel _____ when I play with my friend.

9. That is a _____ joke.   10. The flower is _____.

SPELL CHAT

Tell a classmate how you look and feel on your birthday. Use two or more spelling words.

Spelling Words	
any	pretty
many	funny
very	sorry
every	story
happy	money

Spelling Words

any	pretty
many	funny
very	sorry
every	story
happy	money

Review	Challenge
great	fantasy
shop	mystery
my	

My Words

Quick Write

How do you get to school from home? Write the first three steps you take.

PROOFREADING MARKS

∧ Add
◯ Check spelling
— Cross out
≡ Capital letter

Ⓐ Write Three Rules

Think about your favourite game. Write the first three rules. Use two or more spelling words.

You may do this activity on a computer.

Ⓑ Proofread

Rosa wrote about a game. She found two mistakes. Find four more mistakes that Rosa made, and fix them.

My

Ⓜⓘ Favourite Game

Here's how to play this grate game.
                rolls
1. Someone ~~roll~~ a big ball.

2. The ball comes vere fast.

3. Ever child kick the ball.

Proofread the rules you wrote.
Check your spelling.

Spelling Tip
Add **-s** to an action word that tells about one person, place, or thing. Do not add **-s** if the action word tells about more than one.

A Use the Dictionary: **Example Sentence**

Sometimes an example sentence follows a definition. The sentence shows how the word is used.

any
adjective One or more.
Do you have any brothers or sisters?

Write your own sentence, using the word **any**.

1. _____

B Test Yourself

The spelling words below are written in code.
Cross out every other letter, starting with the first.
Write the word spelled by the letters that are left.

2. a s o t b o q r u y
   _____

3. u p t r m e n t b t d y
   _____

4. e v i e y r p y
   _____

5. b e s v o e r r c y
   _____

6. c m w a c n r y
   _____

7. t a q n e y
   _____

8. x m o o m n i e n y
   _____

9. p s r o v r c r t y
   _____

10. g f m u l n p n o y
    _____

11. j h z a y p n p r y
    _____

Get Word Wise

Any and **every** can be joined with **body**, **one**, and **thing**. How many words can you make?

For Tomorrow

 See the word.

 Say it slowly.

Link sounds and letters.

Write.

Check.

Share What words ending with y did you find?

Spelling Words	
any	pretty
many	funny
very	sorry
every	story
happy	money

Spelling Words

all	tall
ball	wall
call	talk
fall	walk
hall	shall

LOOKOUT WORD

Review	Challenge
push	chalkboard
much	beanstalk
will	

My Words

Words With /ô/

I like tall talk!

A See and Say

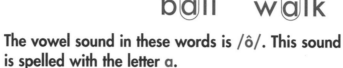

all   talk
ball   walk

The vowel sound in these words is /ô/. This sound is spelled with the letter a.

B Link Sounds and Letters
Sort the spelling words. Write them on the lines.

Words With -all

1. _____   5. _____   8. _____

Words With -alk

2. _____   6. _____

3. _____   7. _____   9. _____

10. _____

4. _____

C Write and Check
Find the two **-all** words in the riddle. Write the words on the lines.

11. _____   12. _____

Riddle
Where will I be if I fall?

off the wall

Name ....

A Make New Words

Change the underlined letter in each word to make a spelling word. Write the word.

1. i_l_l _____

2. w_e_ll _____

3. cal_f_ _____

4. fai_l_ _____

5. hi_l_l _____

6. tai_l_ _____

7. b_e_ll _____

8. sh_e_ll _____

9. ta_n_k _____

10. _t_alk _____

B Common Phrases

Write a spelling word to finish each phrase.

11. down the _____

12. give a _____

13. take a _____

14. make a _____

Be a Spelling Sleuth

Look at a poster for words with the sound /ô/, such as **ball** and **call**.

SPELL CHAT

Talk with a friend about things you like to see as the seasons change. Use two or more spelling words.

Spelling Words	
all	tall
ball	wall
call	talk
fall	walk
hall	shall

Name

Quick Write

Write two sentences telling what places you like to visit. Use two or more spelling words.

A **Write About a Place**

Think about a museum you have visited. What did you see inside? Write a few sentences about it. Use two or more spelling words.

 You may do this activity on a computer.

B **Proofread**

SuCha wrote about her favourite museum. She found two mistakes. Find four more mistakes that SuCha made, and fix them.

Tip
Remember to use the correct words in the naming part of a sentence.

I like the dinosaurs at the museum very
much
mush. ~~It~~ They are fun to see. I can wak al

around the hal of dinosaurs. One day

two dinosaurs fell down! It made such

a loud noise.   SuCha

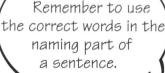

Proofread your sentences. Check your spelling. Make sure you used the correct words in the naming part of the sentences.

Name . . . .

Ⓐ Use the Dictionary: Two Definitions

A definition tells what a word means. Some words have more than one meaning. Circle the second definition.

fall
   1. *verb* To drop to the ground. *Snow falls.*
   2. *noun* The season between summer and winter.

Write the spelling word for the definition.

   1. *verb* To give someone or something a name.
   2. *verb* To shout something out, especially someone's name.

1. _____

Ⓑ Test Yourself

The letters and numbers form a code. Solve each code to write a spelling word.

a	b	c	f	h	k	l	s	t	w
0	1	2	3	4	5	6	7	8	9

2. 74066 _____

3. 8066 _____

4. 9066 _____

5. 8065 _____

6. 066 _____

7. 2066 _____

8. 1066 _____

9. 3066 _____

10. 9065 _____

11. 4066 _____

Get Word Wise

If you start something, you might say you **get the ball rolling**.

For Tomorrow

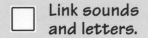 See the word.

 Say it slowly.

 Link sounds and letters.

▽ Write.

⬣ Check.

Share What words with /ô/ did you find?

Spelling Words

all	tall
ball	wall
call	talk
fall	walk
hall	shall

Name..

The Names of Places

Write a spelling word to finish each sentence.

have   each   easy   all

Every town, city, and place has a name. But __(1)__ you ever wondered where __(2)__ name comes from? Names like Green Hill and Pleasant Valley are __(3)__ to figure out. The name tells what the place is like. But not __(4)__ names are like that.

same   name   many

You are now entering Kingston

Some places have the __(5)__ name. You can find the __(6)__ Kingston in __(7)__ provinces.

today   funny   story

Some places have __(8)__ names, like Moose Jaw and Sleepy Eye. There is often a __(9)__ behind names like these. If you could give your town a name __(10)__, what would you call it?

1.

2.

3.

4.

5.

6.

7.

8.

9.

10.

Action-Packed Words

Write a spelling word to finish each saying.

play   wake   walk   feel   fall

1. _____ up early

2. take a _____

3. _____ better

4. trip and _____

5. _____ ball

Word Clues

Write the spelling word that matches each clue.

afraid   three   talk   call

6. scared _____

7. speak _____

8. shout _____

9. one plus two _____

Rhyme Time!

Write the spelling word that rhymes
with each clue word.

said   very   need

10. weed _____

11. merry _____

12. bread _____

Name . . . .

No Place Like It

Write about a town. Use as many spelling words as you can. Then draw a picture.

Tip
Remember to begin the name of a town with a capital letter.

name	easy
have	very
place	every
away	all
play	fall
three	walk

1. Come visit _____ .

2. You can _____ .

3. Your children can _____

4. The best thing about this town is _____

_____ .

Look at the words you spelled wrong on your Unit 3 Post-Tests. Use some to write a sentence that tells about your town.

5. _____

Proofread your sentence. Make sure your spelling, capitalization, and end marks are correct.

Brag About It . . . .

Write a sentence asking a friend to visit your town.

6. _____

PROOFREADING MARKS

∧ Add
◯ Check spelling
— Cross out
≡ Capital letter

Name . . . .

Write It Right
Read each sentence. Circle the word that is spelled wrong.
Write it correctly.

play   many   story   every   funny   afraid   place   away

1. Mne people think spelling is hard. _____

2. Not evre word is hard to spell. _____

3. A word may have a fune spelling. _____

Spelling Matters!

4. Some letters may be in a strange plas. _____

5. Sometimes you have to take a letter awa. _____

6. Don't be afrad of that! _____

7. What spelling words are in the storee? _____

8. Use the words to write a pla . _____

Spelling Words

nice	slide
nine	smile
fine	time
line	write
side	live LOOKOUT WORD

Review	Challenge
shall	sidewalk
stick	crocodile
like	

My Words

_____

_____

_____

_____

_____

Learn and Spell   Name . . . .

Words With Long i

> Live animals live here.

A **See and Say**   fine   smile
nice   write

These words have the long i sound.
This vowel sound is spelled i-consonant-e.

HOME

B **Link Sounds and Letters**
Sort the spelling words. Write them on the lines.

-ide
1. _____
2. _____

-ice
3. _____

-ile
4. _____

-ite
5. _____

-ime
6. _____

-ine
7. _____
8. _____
9. _____

-ive
10. _____

C **Write and Check**
Write a spelling word to answer the riddle.

_____

11. _____

Riddle
If three is a crowd, what are four and five?

Ⓐ Word Ladder
Copy the top word. Then follow the directions to write more spelling words.

1. **nice** _____

Change the _____

2. **c** to **n** _____

3. first **n** to **f** _____

4. **f** to **l** _____

5. **live** _____

Change the _____

6. **l** to **s**,
   v to **d** _____

7. **s** to **sm**,
   d to **l** _____

8. **sm** to **t**,
   l to **m** _____

Ⓑ Action Words
Sometimes you have to change the spelling
of a word to tell about the past.

9. I will _____ Tim a letter now.

10. I _____ Tim a letter last week.

11. Please help me _____ this box over here.

12. Last night, I _____ the box over here.

Now	Past
write	wrote
slide	slid

Be a Spelling Sleuth
Look in books for three
words with the long i sound,
such as **line**.

SPELL CHAT

What things make
you smile? Name five
things with a friend.

Spelling Words	
nice	slide
nine	smile
fine	time
line	write
side	live

Name . . . .

Spelling Words

nice	slide
nine	smile
fine	time
line	write
side	live

Review	Challenge
shall	sidewalk
stick	crocodile
like	

My Words

Quick Write

Write a few sentences about someone you like. Tell why you like him or her. Use two or more spelling words.

A Write About a Character

Imagine that you are your favourite folk tale character. Write about yourself. Use two or more spelling words.

 You may do this activity on a computer.

B Proofread

Kate wrote these sentences to tell what Little Red Hen is like. She found two mistakes. Find four more mistakes that Kate made, and fix them.

Little Red Hen

i work hard. I try to be nis. I lik my

friends. They say they do not have tiem

to help me. this does not make me smiel.

by Kate

Proofread your writing. Check your spelling. Be sure that each sentence begins with a capital letter.

Tip
Always begin the first word of a sentence with a capital letter.

PROOFREADING MARKS

∧ Add
◯ Check spelling
ℓ Take out
≡ Capital letter

Name . . . .

A Use the Dictionary: Guide Words

Look for guide words at the top of a dictionary page.
Guide words tell the first and last words on that page.

---

smell ▶ snag

smell 1. *verb* To sense an odour with your nose. *I can smell dinner cooking.*

smoke 1. *noun* The mixture of gas and tiny carbon particles that is given off when something burns.

smog *noun* A mixture of fog and smoke that sometimes hangs in the air over cities and industrial areas.

snag 1. *noun* A small, unexpected problem or difficulty **2.** *verb* To catch on something. *I snagged my sleeve on a nail.*

---

1. What spelling word is on this dictionary page? _____

B Test Yourself

Write a spelling word for each definition.

2. good _____

3. kind _____

4. to be alive _____

5. a long, thin mark _____

6. not front or back _____

7. opposite of **frown** _____

8. move smoothly _____

9. the number after 8 _____

10. put words on paper _____

11. what a clock shows _____

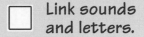

Name ....

Spelling Words

high	right
light	bright
fight	sight
might	tight
night	eight

LOOKOUT WORD

Review	Challenge
live	midnight
wake	sunlight
fly	

My Words

More Words With Long i

E-i- e-i- eight!

A **See and Say**   h igh   l ight

n ight   br ight

These words have the long i sound.
This vowel sound is spelled with the letters igh.

B Link Sounds and Letters

Sort the spelling words. Write them on the lines.

Consonant + igh + t

1. _____   5. _____

2. _____   6. _____

3. _____   7. _____

4. _____   8. _____

Vowel + igh + t

9. _____

Consonant + igh

10. _____

C Write and Check

Write two words in the button with the long i sound.

11. _____   12. _____

Riddle
What can go right through water and not get wet?
ᴉɥƃᴉl

Name ....

A Word Meaning

Write a spelling word for each clue.

1. not left _____

2. 1 + 7 = ___ _____

3. not dark _____

4. not loose _____

5. begins like **fun**, rhymes with **kite** _____

6. not day _____

7. ability to see _____

8. not dull _____

9. not low _____

10. begins like **mud**, rhymes with **bite** _____

B Words With -er and -est

Add **-er** to a describing word to compare two things.
Add **-est** to compare more than two things.
Write **high**, **higher**, or **highest** in each sentence.

11. See how _____ you can throw the ball.

12. Anika can throw a ball _____ than I can.

13. Juan throws it the _____ of all.

Be a Spelling Sleuth

Look in stores for three words with the long i sound, such as **light**.

SPELL CHAT

With a friend, make up sentences using the words **bright**, **brighter**, **brightest**.

Spelling Words

high	right
light	bright
fight	sight
might	tight
night	eight

Spelling Words

high	right
light	bright
fight	sight
might	tight
night	eight

Review	Challenge
live	midnight
wake	sunlight
fly	

My Words

Quick Write

Draw the night sky. Label the things you drew in your picture. Use two or more spelling words.

PROOFREADING MARKS

∧ Add
◯ Check spelling
ℓ Take out
☰ Capital letter

A **Write a Poem**

Use four spelling words to finish the poem "Night."

 You may do this activity on a computer.

It was late at _____,

The stars I saw were _____.

Then I saw another _____,

One small ship with one big _____.

B **Proofread**

Yoshi wrote a poem. He found two mistakes. Find four more mistakes that Yoshi made, and fix them.

> Stars by Yoshi
> night
> Stars in the (nit).
> shine
> They shines very brite.
>
> When I wak in the light,
>
> The stars twinkles out of sigth .

Tip
The naming part and the doing part of your sentences must work together.

Proofread the poem you finished. Check your spelling.

Name...

A Use the Dictionary: Idioms

Sometimes a group of words means something different from what it says. "It's raining cats and dogs" doesn't mean that animals are falling from the sky. It means it's raining very hard.

light

1. *verb* To start something burning. ▷ *noun* light 2. If you **see the light**, you understand something for the first time.

idiom

What is the girl saying?

_____

_____

1. I see the _____.

B Test Yourself

Fill in the missing letters to write spelling words.

2. h_ _ _ _

3. e_ _ _ _

4. l_ _ _ _

5. m_ _ _ _

6. s_ _ _ _ _

7. f_ _ _ _

8. r_ _ _ _

9. b_ _ _ _ _

10. t_ _ _ _

11. n_ _ _ _

For Tomorrow

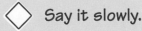 See the word.

◇ Say it slowly.

□ Link sounds and letters.

▽ Write.

⬡ Check.

Share What long i words did you find?

Spelling Words	
high	right
light	bright
fight	sight
might	tight
night	eight

Spelling Words

boat	toad
coat	soak
goat	soap
float	toast
road	most LOOKOUT WORD

Review	Challenge
eight	koala
today	roller coaster
rode	

My Words

Words With Long o

The letter I like most is o.

A **See and Say**   coat road
float toast

These words have the long o sound.
This vowel sound is spelled with the letters oa.

Memory Jogger

B **Link Sounds and Letters**
Sort the spelling words. Write them on the lines.

-oat

1. _____

2. _____

3. _____

4. _____

-oad

5. _____

6. _____

-oak

7. _____

-oap

8. _____

-oast

9. _____

-ost

10. _____

C **Write and Check**
Which two words in the riddle have the long o sound? Write them.

11. _____   12. _____

Riddle
Why did the toad cross the road?

to get to the other side

Name . . . .

Ⓐ Puzzle Clues
Write the spelling word that goes with each clue.

1. It looks like a frog.

2. This means "to keep wet."

3. This animal is like a sheep.

4. This is the opposite of **least**.

5. A boat does this.

6. What spelling word is in the boxes? _____

Ⓑ Naming Words
A noun is a word that names a person, place, or thing.

 girl   **school**   **kite**

Write the spelling word that names each picture.

7. _____

9. _____

8. _____

10. _____

Words With Long *o* 89

Be a Spelling Sleuth
Look in magazines for three words with the long o sound spelled oa, as in **boat**.

SPELL CHAT

Tell a friend about something that can float. Use two or more spelling words.

Spelling Words	
boat	toad
coat	soak
goat	soap
float	toast
road	most

Name . . . .

Spelling Words

boat	toad
coat	soak
goat	soap
float	toast
road	most

Review	Challenge
eight	koala
today	roller coaster
rode	

My Words

Quick Write

Draw and label pictures of three animal characters. Use two or more spelling words.

Ⓐ Write About a Character

What is your favourite animal character? Write one question to ask that character. Then write the answer. Use two or more spelling words.

You may do this activity on a computer.

Ⓑ Proofread

Chen wrote a story about Rabbit and Toad. She found two mistakes. Find four more mistakes that Chen made, and fix them.

> **Tip**
> A telling sentence ends with a period. An asking sentence ends with a question mark.

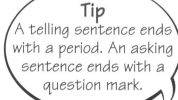

Rabbit asked Toad, "How wet
~~today~~
was it (tooday)?"

Toad said it was very wet. "Did you

see me flot in a bote down the rod "

by Chen

Now proofread your story. Check your spelling. Make sure each sentence has an ending mark.

PROOFREADING MARKS

∧ Add
◯ Check spelling
ℓ Take out
≡ Capital letter

Name ....

A Use the Dictionary: Word History

Would it surprise you to learn that words have histories? They do. You will find word histories in special boxes in the dictionary.

soap *noun* A substance used for washing and cleaning.

soap opera *noun* A television series about the tangled loves and lives of a group of people.

Word History

The term **soap opera** dates back to 1939, when *Newsweek* magazine used it to tell about the 15-minute plays then on the radio. *Newsweek* used the word *opera* because the plays were like short operas. The name *soap* was used because companies that made soap sponsored many of these programs.

Circle the word history box. What spelling word does the word history box tell about?

1. _____

B Test Yourself

Write spelling words by filling in the missing letters.

2. p

3. c

4. s

5. t

6. b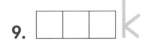

7. r

8. d

9. k

10. g

11. f

Spelling Words

old	told
cold	bold
gold	sold
hold	scold
fold	roll *LOOKOUT WORD*

Review	Challenge
most	troll
dream	stroll
hope	

My Words

_____

_____

_____

_____

Learn and Spell   Name ....

More Words With Long o

Ⓐ See and Say

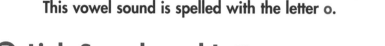

It's **oh** so **old**!

These words have the long o sound followed by ld. This vowel sound is spelled with the letter o.

Ⓑ Link Sounds and Letters

Sort the spelling words. Write them on the lines.

-old

1. _____   4. _____   7. _____

2. _____   5. _____   8. _____

3. _____   6. _____   9. _____

LOOKOUT WORD

10. _____

Ⓒ Write and Check

Write the spelling words in the comic strip that have the long **o** sound.

11. _____   12. _____

Put on this coat.   No!   I have a cold.   I told you so!

Name . . . .

Ⓐ Describing Words

Write the spelling word that could describe each picture.

1. _____

2. _____

3. _____

4. _____

Ⓑ Action Words

Write a spelling word to finish each sentence.

5. Will you _____ my hand?

6. If the dog eats your lunch, _____ him.

7. _____ the paper in half like this.

8. I saw the pen _____ off the table.

9. Sara _____ me a funny story.

10. Josh _____ his old bike.

SPELL CHAT

With a friend, name something **old**. Then name something **cold** or **gold**.

Spelling Words	
old	told
cold	bold
gold	sold
hold	scold
fold	roll

Spelling Words

old	told
cold	bold
gold	sold
hold	scold
fold	roll

Review	Challenge
most	troll
dream	stroll
hope	

My Words

_____
_____
_____
_____

Quick Write

Who are your favourite story characters? Write about how they are alike. Use two or more spelling words.

Name ....

A Make a Poster
What is your favourite story? Make a poster that tells about it. Use two or more spelling words.

 You may do this activity on a computer.

B Proofread
Liz wrote about her favourite story for a poster. She found two mistakes. Find four more mistakes that Liz made, and fix them.

Tip
Remember to write your sentences carefully. The words must be in an order that makes sense.

Liz

Frog and Toad Are Friends

This is story about old friends.

Frog and Toad went swimming.

Toad tol Frog he was cld.

I hopp you the like story!

Proofread your writing. Check your spelling. Make sure your words are in the right order.

PROOFREADING MARKS
- ∧ Add
- ◯ Check spelling
- ℓ Take out
- ≡ Capital letter

Name ....

Ⓐ Use the Dictionary: Homophones

Words that sound alike but have different spellings and meanings are called homophones. You can find homophones at the end of a dictionary entry.

> **roll**
> 1. *verb* To move along by turning over and over. *The ball rolled down the hill.*
> 2. *verb* To make something into the shape of a ball or tube. *Charlie rolled the clay into balls.*
> **Roll** sounds like **role.**
> ▷*verb* **rolling, rolled** ▷*noun* **roll**

Write the two homophones in this entry.

1. _____   2. _____

Ⓑ Test Yourself

Write a spelling word for each clue.

3. carry something _____

4. sc + told - t _____

5. yellow colour _____

6. to bend _____

7. said _____

8. traded for money _____

9. not young _____

10. not hot _____

11. not shy _____

12. turn over and over _____

Get Word Wise

The word **roll** comes from a Latin word that means "small wheel."

For Tomorrow

 See the word.

 Say it slowly.

 Link sounds and letters.

▽ Write.

⬡ Check.

Share What long o words did you find?

Spelling Words	
old	told
cold	bold
gold	sold
hold	scold
fold	roll

Spelling Words

own	snow
low	throw
blow	window
grow	yellow
show	hello *LOOKOUT WORD*

Review	Challenge
roll	shadow
money	snowflake
go	

My Words

Other Words With Long o

A **See and Say**   low   show   grow   yellow

These words have the long o sound.
This vowel sound is spelled with the letters ow.

Window begins and ends with **w**.

B **Link Sounds and Letters**
Sort the spelling words. Write them on the lines.

Three Letters

1. _____

2. _____

Four Letters

3. _____

4. _____

5. _____

6. _____

Five Letters

7. _____

8. _____

Six Letters

9. _____

10. _____

C **Write and Check**
Answer the riddle with two spelling words.
Write the words on the lines.

11. a _____ _____

Riddle
What do you call dancing flakes?

Name . . . .

A Make New Words

Change the underlined letter or letters to make a
spelling word. Write the word on the line.

1. g<u>l</u>ow _____

2. ow<u>l</u> _____

3. b<u>l</u>o<u>t</u> _____

4. thr<u>ew</u> _____

5. <u>f</u>ellow _____

6. l<u>a</u>w _____

7. sho<u>p</u> _____

8. s<u>l</u>ow _____

9. hel<u>ps</u> _____

10. wind<u>ed</u> _____

B Action Words

The spelling of these words changes to tell about the past.

grow → grew   throw → threw   blow → blew

Write a word that tells about the past to finish each sentence.

11. Last summer I _____ beans in my garden.

12. Jamal _____ the ball to me.

13. Amy and I _____ out all the candles.

Be a Spelling Sleuth

Look in poems for three
words with the long o sound
spelled ow, such as **snow**
and **blow**.

SPELL CHAT

Tell a classmate
what you would like
to see outside your
classroom window. Use
two or more spelling
words.

Spelling Words	
own	snow
low	throw
blow	window
grow	yellow
show	hello

Spelling Words

own	snow
low	throw
blow	window
grow	yellow
show	hello

Review	Challenge
roll	shadow
money	snowflake
go	

My Words

Quick Write

Why do you think people like to grow things? Write one reason. Use two or more spelling words.

A Write a Story

Draw a picture of a window box garden. Write a sentence about your garden. Use one or more spelling words.

You may do this activity on a computer.

B Proofread

Oscar wrote about his window garden. He found two mistakes. Find four more mistakes that Oscar made, and fix them.

Oscar

I want to sho you the windo garden

that I grew. It has yello , red, and blue

money

flowers. I got it with my own muney

Tip
Remember to write an ending mark for each sentence.

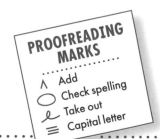

PROOFREADING MARKS

∧ Add

○ Check spelling

ℓ Take out

≡ Capital letter

Proofread your sentences. Check your spelling. Be sure every sentence has an ending mark.

Study and Review Name . . . .

Ⓐ Use the Dictionary: **Word Endings**

Many words can be used with different endings.
When you look up a word, go to the end of the entry
to find the word with different endings. The new
words are in dark type.

> **show**
> 1. *verb* To let see or be seen. *Show me the picture. Show the book to them.*
> 2. *verb* To explain or demonstrate to someone. *Show me how to do it.*
> ▷ *verb* **showing, showed**

Write **show** with two different endings.

1. _____   2. _____

Ⓑ Test Yourself

Fill in the missing letters to write spelling words.

3. o___ ___

4. ___ h ___ ___

5. g ___ ___ ___

6. ___ o ___
    ___ l

7. ___ ___ l ___

8. ___ e ___ ___ ___

9. y ___ ___ ___ ___
    ___ h ___

10. ___ ___ h ___ ___

11. s ___ ___ ___

12. ___ ___ n ___ w

Get Word Wise

The word **window** is
from two words from
Norway that mean
"wind" and "eye."

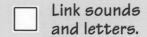

For Tomorrow

 ▷ See the word.

◇ Say it slowly.

☐ Link sounds
   and letters.

▽ Write.

⬡ Check.

Share What long *o* words
spelled *ow* did you find?

Spelling Words	
own	snow
low	throw
blow	window
grow	yellow
show	hello

Name . . . .

Your Dog's Best Friend Is You

Write a spelling word to finish each sentence.

time   live   right   show

You must learn what it's like to __(1)__ with a
new puppy. It takes __(2)__ to train him. __(3)__ him
what you want. He wants to do what's __(4)__ .

coat   own   grow

When you __(5)__ a puppy, you must take care
of him. You must feed him and help him __(6)__ . You
must keep his furry __(7)__ clean and brushed.
You must not let him run in the road.

night   most   cold

A puppy needs a place to run and play. At __(8)__ ,
he needs a place to sleep. He should stay inside
when it's __(9)__ . __(10)__ of all, a puppy needs love.

1. _____

2. _____

3. _____

4. _____

5. _____

6. _____

7. _____

8. _____

9. _____

10. _____

Word Pairs

Some words go together, like **milk** and **cookies**.
Write spelling words that go with these words.

soap   yellow   toast
hello   old

1. _____ and jam

2. _____ and water

3. blue and _____

4. _____ and wise

5. _____ and how are you

Old Sayings...

Write a spelling word to finish each saying.

side   light   nine   hold

6. _____ as a feather

7. _____, ten, start again

8. _____ your horses

9. side by _____

Word Ladder................

Go from **hole** to **told** in
two steps. Change only
one letter at a time.

10. hole

11. _____

12. _____

Name ....

Helpful Hints

Write a sentence to solve each problem.
Use spelling words in your sentences.

Tip
Always begin the first word of a sentence with a capital letter.

time	hold
light	roll
night	own
coat	grow
soap	show
old	yellow

1. Your puppy cries at night.

_____

_____

2. Your puppy chews on shoes.

_____

_____

3. Your puppy rolled in a mud puddle.

_____

_____

4. Your puppy eats another puppy's food.

_____

_____

Look at the words you spelled wrong on your Unit 4 Post-Tests.
Use some of them to tell about a trick your puppy knows.

_____

5. _____

Make a Wish ....

Write a sentence about a pet you would like to have.

_____

6. _____

Proofread your sentence. Make sure your spelling, capitalization, and end marks are correct.

PROOFREADING MARKS
....
∧ Add
◯ Check spelling
ℓ Take out
≡ Capital letter

Name ....

Words That Sound Alike

Read each pair of sentences. Write a word that sounds like the underlined word to finish the second sentence.

road   write   high   eight   roll

1. Juanita said <u>hi</u> when she saw me.

I lifted my hand _____ to wave to her.

2. Think of the <u>right</u> words to say.

Then _____ a note to your friend.

3. Everyone <u>ate</u> two rolls.

There were _____ rolls left.

4. Tina <u>rode</u> her bike.

The _____ was beside the river.

5. Jim plays the <u>role</u> of a catcher.

The balls _____ to him.

Spelling Matters!

Name ....

Words With /ōō/

Spelling Words

blue	rule
glue	huge
true	sure
cute	use
tube	shoes LOOKOUT WORD

Review	Challenge
hello	parachute
talk	cruel
do	

My Words

_____

_____

_____

_____

A **See and Say**

blue   tube
true   rule

The vowel sound in these words is /ōō/.
The sound is spelled **ue** or **u-consonant-e**.

I need a huge hug!

B **Link Sounds and Letters**
Sort the spelling words. Write them on the lines.

u-consonant-e

1. _____

2. _____

3. _____

4. _____

5. _____

6. _____

oe

7. _____

ue

8. _____

9. _____

10. _____

C **Write and Check**
Find three words in the poem that have /ōō/.
Write the two spelling words.

11. _____

12. _____

*Poem
Red, white,
and blue,
Bright colours
true.
I love you.*

A Make New Words
Change one letter in each word to make a spelling word. Write the new word.

1. role _____

2. shops _____

3. sore _____

4. glee _____

Add one letter to each word to make a spelling word.

5. us _____

6. tub _____

B Describing Words
A describing word can tell how something looks, sounds, or feels. It can also tell what something is like. Finish each sentence with a spelling word that describes.

7. What a _____ kitten!

8. The dog has a _____ bone.

9. The girl has a _____ cap.

10. This is a _____ story.

Be a Spelling Sleuth
Look in a newspaper for at least three words with /ōō/, such as **blue**.

SPELL CHAT

Ask a classmate to use a spelling word to describe a pet. Is it **cute**? Is it **huge**?

Spelling Words	
blue	rule
glue	huge
true	sure
cute	use
tube	shoes

Spelling Words

blue	rule
glue	huge
true	sure
cute	use
tube	shoes

Review	Challenge
hello	parachute
talk	cruel
do	

My Words

Quick Write

Think of some rules in your school. Make a list of three rules. Use two or more spelling words.

A Write a Class Rule

Write a class rule that will help everyone. Tell why that rule is important. Use at least one spelling word.

 You may do this activity on a computer.

B Proofread

Meg wrote a rule for her class to use. She found two mistakes. Find four more mistakes that Meg made, and fix them.

Spelling Tip
A contraction is two words made into one shorter word. Use an ' to take the place of missing letters.

Meg   Class Rule #3

Don't take another student's gloo.

Doo use your own.

This makes sher youw'll have glue

when you need it.

PROOFREADING MARKS

∧   Add
◯   Check spelling
ℓ   Take out
≡   Capital letter

Now proofread your class rules. Check your spelling. Make sure you write contractions correctly.

Name . . . .

A Use the Dictionary: Example Sentences

Sometimes an example sentence follows the meaning of a word. The sentence shows how the word is used.

Write the example sentence from the dictionary entry. Circle the spelling word.

blue
1. *noun* The colour of the sky on a sunny day. 2. *adjective* Sad. *Winter makes me blue.*

1. _____

B Test Yourself

Use the secret code to write spelling words.

| b | c | e | g | h | l | o | r | s | t | u |

2. _____

3. _____

4. _____

5. _____

6. _____

7. _____

8. _____

9. _____

10. _____

11. _____

Get Word Wise

TVs have picture tubes inside. That's why we sometimes say we're watching the "tube."

For Tomorrow

 See the word.

 Say it slowly.

☐ Link sounds and letters.

▽ Write.

⬡ Check.

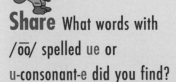

Share What words with /o͞o/ spelled ue or u-consonant-e did you find?

Spelling Words

blue	rule
glue	huge
true	sure
cute	use
tube	shoes

Name ....

Another Spelling for /o͞o/

Don't forget the *e* in sew. Think: It's *easy* to sew.

A **See and Say**   drew   new
grew   chew

These words end with /o͞o/.
This vowel sound is spelled with the letters ew.

B **Link Sounds and Letters**
Sort the spelling words. Write them on the lines.

Memory Jogger

Spelling Words

dew	flew
few	drew
new	grew
chew	threw
blew	sew

LOOKOUT WORD

Review	Challenge
shoes	newspaper
write	view
so	

My Words

/o͞o/ Spelled With ew

1. _____   5. _____   9. _____

2. _____   6. _____

Long o Spelled With ew

10. _____

3. _____   7. _____

4. _____   8. _____

C **Write and Check**
Which words in the riddle rhyme?
Write the two spelling words.

11. _____   12. _____

Riddle
What did the bubble do as the girl blew?

It grew.

Vocabulary Practice   Name .....

A Homophones
Write the spelling word that sounds the same as the underlined word.

pear

pair

_____

1. Kyle _____ the ball <u>through</u> the window.

2. These pants are <u>so</u> torn that I can't _____ them.

3. I <u>knew</u> I would get a _____ hat!

4. The wind _____ away my <u>blue</u> hat!

B Past-Time Action Words
The spelling of some words changes to tell about the past. Write past-time spelling words.

6. blow _____   8. grow _____

7. draw _____   9. fly _____

C Write

10. I mean "not many." What word am I? _____

Be a Spelling Sleuth
Look in books for three words with /ōō/ spelled ew, such as **flew**.

SPELL CHAT

Work with a friend. Think of two words that sound the same but have different meanings. Use a spelling word.

Spelling Words

dew	flew
few	drew
new	grew
chew	threw
blew	sew

Name . . . .

Spelling Words

dew	flew
few	drew
new	grew
chew	threw
blew	sew

Review	Challenge
shoes	newspaper
write	view
so	

My Words

Quick Write

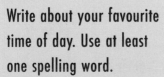

Write about your favourite time of day. Use at least one spelling word.

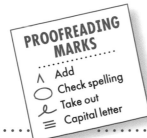

PROOFREADING MARKS

∧   Add
◯   Check spelling
ℓ   Take out
=   Capital letter

110   Lesson 26

Ⓐ Write in a Journal

Write in your journal. Tell about something that happened to you early one morning. Use two or more spelling words.

You may do this activity on a computer.

Ⓑ Proofread

Pete wrote in his journal. He found two mistakes. Find four more mistakes, and fix them.

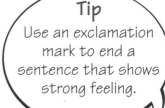

Tip
Use an exclamation mark to end a sentence that shows strong feeling.

Friday

This morning was fun! I got out of

                               flew

bed so fast. I almost ⓕⓛⓤ. I put on my nu

shues . I throo my old ones away.

It felt great

Now proofread what you wrote. Check your spelling. Did you end each sentence correctly?

Name . . . .

Ⓐ Use the Dictionary: Guide Words

The words at the top of a dictionary page are called guide words. They tell the first and last words on the page.

Look at the guide words. Write the spelling word that you would find on each dictionary page.

cheese ▶ chicken	fern ▶ fib

1. _____ 2. _____

Ⓑ Test Yourself

Write the spelling word that begins with the same sound or sounds as each picture name.

 3. _____

 4. _____

 5. _____

 6. _____

 7. _____

 8. _____

 9. _____

3 10. _____

 11. _____

 12. _____

Get Word Wise

The word **homophone** comes from two Greek words that mean "same" and "sound."

For Tomorrow

➡ See the word.

◇ Say it slowly.

☐ Link sounds and letters.

▽ Write.

⬢ Check.

Share What words with /o͞o/ spelled ew did you find?

Spelling Words	
dew	flew
few	drew
new	grew
chew	threw
blew	sew

Spelling Words

book	wood
cook	stood
look	would
took	could
good	should

LOOKOUT WORDS

Review	Challenge
sew	good night
right	notebook
bad	

My Words

Words With /o͞o/

A **See and Say**   look could book would

The letters oo or ou can stand for the vowel sound /o͞o/.

B **Link Sounds and Letters**

Sort the spelling words. Write them on the lines.

oo

1. _____ 5. _____

2. _____ 6. _____

3. _____ 7. _____

4. _____

ou

8. _____

9. _____

10. _____

C **Write and Check**

Read the button. Which two spelling words sound the same but have different spellings? Write them.

11. _____ 12. _____

Look for /o͞o/ in a book.

Memory Jogger

How much wood would a woodchuck chuck if a woodchuck could chuck wood?

Name ....

A Word Puzzles
Write the spelling word for each clue.

1. Rhymes with **wood** and starts like _____

2. Rhymes with **should** and starts like _____

3. Rhymes with **could** and starts like _____

4. Rhymes with **good** and starts like _____

B Rhyming Words
Say all the words in a group. Write the two that rhyme.

book   stood   cook

5. _____

6. _____

book   good   wood

7. _____

8. _____

look   took   should

9. _____

10. _____

could   would   look

11. _____

12. _____

Be a Spelling Sleuth
Look at signs to find two or more words spelled with /o͝o/, such as **look**.

SPELL CHAT

With a friend, make up a short sentence, using the words **wood** and **would**.

Spelling Words	
book	wood
cook	stood
look	would
took	could
good	should

Spelling Words

book	wood
cook	stood
look	would
took	could
good	should

Review	Challenge
sew	good night
right	notebook
bad	

My Words

Quick Write

Do you help care for a pet or a baby? List some things you could do. Use two or more spelling words.

You may do this activity on a computer.

A Write a Note

You are going away. Your friend will take care of your plants. Write a note telling how to care for your plants. Use two spelling words.

B Proofread

Kuni wrote a note to his friend Adam. He found two mistakes. Find four more mistakes, and fix them.

Tip
Remember to write your sentences carefully. The words must be in an order that makes sense.

Dear Adam,

We be will ^be^ gone for one week. I wish you ⟨wood⟩ ^would^ luk at our plants each day.

You shuld water them they if look bd.

Thanks,

Kuni

PROOFREADING MARKS
∧ Add
◯ Check spelling
ℓ Take out
☰ Capital letter

Now proofread the note you wrote. Check your spelling. Did you write words in the correct order?

Name . . . .

Ⓐ Use the Dictionary: **Word Endings**

A word can have one or more different endings. Find the words in dark type at the end of the second definition. Write the new words.

book

1. *noun* A set of pages that are bound together in a cover. 2. *verb* To arrange for something ahead of time. *We've booked a vacation in Mexico.* ▷ **booking, booked**

1. _____

2. _____

Ⓑ Test Yourself

Fill in the missing letters to make a spelling word.

3. b_____ _____ _____

4. W_____ _____ _____

5. t_____ _____ _____

6. C_____ _____ _____

7. g_____ _____ _____

8. l_____ _____ _____

9. W_____ _____ _____

10. S_____ _____ _____

11. C_____ _____ _____

12. S_____ _____ _____

Get Word Wise

Your **foot** is at the end of your leg. Where do you think the **foot** of your bed is?

For Tomorrow

⟹ See the word.

◇ Say it slowly.

☐ Link sounds and letters.

▽ Write.

⬢ Check.

Share What /o͞o/ words did you find?

Spelling Words	
book	wood
cook	stood
look	would
took	could
good	should

Spelling Words

too	moon
food	soon
boot	pool
room	school
broom	two

LOOKOUT WORD

Review	Challenge
would	schoolyard
boat	bathroom
to	

My Words

Name . . . .

More Words With /o͞o/

A **See and Say**   moon   food
broom   p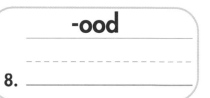ool

The vowel sound in these words is /o͞o/.
The sound is spelled with the letters oo.

The cow jumped over the moon.

B **Link Sounds and Letters**
Sort the spelling words. Write them on the lines.

-oon
1. _____
2. _____

-o
5. _____

-ood
8. _____

-oo
6. _____

-ool
3. _____
4. _____

-oot
7. _____

-oom
9. _____
10. _____

C **Write and Check**
Read the riddle. Write the words with **oo**.

11. _____   12. _____

Riddle
What's another name for a closet?
¡moor moorb A

Vocabulary Practice

Name . . . .

Ⓐ Missing Words

Write a spelling word to finish each sentence.

1. Anna and Kim were _____ hot.

2. They went swimming in the _____ .

3. Anna saw _____ boys eating _____ .

4. _____ the boys left.

5. One boy forgot his _____ .

Ⓑ Make New Words

Change the underlined letter in each word to two letters. Write a spelling word.

6. br<u>i</u>m _____

7. <u>s</u>tool _____

8. s<u>u</u>n _____

9. m<u>a</u>n _____

10. ro<u>w</u> _____

11. <u>p</u>od _____

Be a Spelling Sleuth

Look in stores for three words with /o͞o/ spelled oo, such as **boot**.

SPELL CHAT

Ask a classmate to say a spelling word. Try to find another spelling word that rhymes with it.

Spelling Words	
too	moon
food	soon
boot	pool
room	school
broom	two

Name

Spelling Words

too	moon
food	soon
boot	pool
room	school
broom	two

Review	Challenge
would	schoolyard
boat	bathroom
to	

My Words

Quick Write

Write three things that tell about your school. Use two or three spelling words.

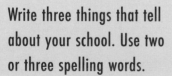

A Write a Description

Write about where you live. What is it like? What makes it special? Use two or more spelling words in your writing.

You may do this activity on a computer.

B Proofread

Maria wrote about where she lives. She found two mistakes. Find four more mistakes that Maria made, and fix them.

Tip
A telling sentence begins with a capital letter and ends with a period.

two
I live to blocks away from schol . It

will be hot here sone. There is a pol in

my town. My friends and I swim there

by Maria

Now proofread your description. Check your spelling. Make sure each telling sentence begins with a capital letter and ends with a period.

PROOFREADING MARKS

∧ Add
◯ Check spelling
ℓ Take out
≡ Capital letter

Study and Review   Name ....

Ⓐ Use the Dictionary: Definition

A definition tells the meaning of a word.
Write the definition for **broom**.

> **broom** *noun*
> A large brush used for sweeping.

1. _____
_____
_____

Ⓑ Test Yourself

Break each code to write a spelling word.

b c d f h l m n o p r s t w

2. _____

3. _____

4. _____

5. _____

6. _____

7. _____

8. _____

9. _____

10. _____

11. _____

More Words With /o͞o/   119

Get Word Wise

A **school** is where you go to learn. Another kind of **school** is a group of fish!

For Tomorrow

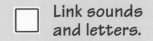 See the word.

Say it slowly.

Link sounds and letters.

Write.

Check.

Share What /o͞o/ words did you find?

Spelling Words

too	moon
food	soon
boot	pool
room	school
broom	two

Spelling Words

out	now
shout	down
loud	town
mouth	brown
how	our **LOOKOUT WORD**

Review	Challenge
two	howl
told	playground
no	

My Words

Words With **ou** and **ow**

*See **ou** in loud mouth.*

A **See and Say**   out   how   mouth   down

The letters **ou** and **ow** often stand for /ou/.
It is the vowel sound you hear in **out** and **how**.

B **Link Sounds and Letters**
Sort the spelling words. Write them on the lines.

-ou

1. _____   3. _____   5. _____

2. _____   4. _____

-ow

6. _____   8. _____   10. _____

7. _____   9. _____

C **Write and Check**
Which four words in the riddle have /ou/? Write the
two that are spelling words.

11. _____   12. _____

Riddle
What did the brown cow shout to the noisy owl?

Don't hoot!

Name . . . .

A Opposites

Write the spelling word that means the opposite of each word.

happy   sad

1. in _____

2. quiet _____

3. whisper _____

4. later _____

5. up _____

B Make New Words

Follow the directions to make a spelling word.

6. Change **c** in **cow** to **h**. _____

7. Change **s** in **south** to **m**. _____

8. Change **g** in **gown** to **t**. _____

9. Change **t** in **out** to **r**. _____

10. Change **cr** in **crown** to **br**. _____

Be a Spelling Sleuth

Look on posters for three words with /ou/ spelled **ou** or **ow**, such as **shout** and **now**.

SPELL CHAT

With a partner, think of a pair of opposites. Use a spelling word.

Spelling Words	
out	now
shout	down
loud	town
mouth	brown
how	our

Spelling Words

out	now
shout	down
loud	town
mouth	brown
how	our

Review	Challenge
two	howl
told	playground
no	

My Words

Quick Write

Write about a place in your city or town that is noisy. Use two or more spelling words.

A Write About a Favourite Place to Play

Write about a place to play. Tell what it looks like. Tell what sounds you hear there. Use spelling words.

You may do this activity on a computer.

B Proofread

Josh wrote this about where he likes to play. He found two mistakes. Find four more mistakes that Josh made, and fix them.

I like the park in our toun. My ~~to~~ two

friends and I have a good time their. We

laugh and (showt) shout when we run dwn the

hill. Sometimes we get very lod.

by Josh

Tip
Some words sound the same but may have very different meanings and spellings. To be sure which spelling is correct, look up the words in a dictionary.

PROOFREADING MARKS
∧ Add
◯ Check spelling
✐ Take out
≡ Capital letter

Proofread your sentences. Check your spelling. Did you spell words that sound alike correctly?

Ⓐ Use the Dictionary: Two Definitions

Some words have more than one definition. Each definition is listed with its own number in the entry.

Write the two definitions for **loud**.

> **loud** *adjective*
> 1. Noisy.
> 2. Very bright and colourful.
> ▷ *adjective* **louder, loudest**

1. _____

2. _____

Ⓑ Test Yourself

Fill in the missing letters to write spelling words.

3. ☐☐t

4. n☐☐

5. o☐☐

6. h☐☐

7. d☐☐☐

8. ☐☐d

9. ☐☐n

10. ☐r☐☐

11. ☐☐☐☐h

12. ☐h☐☐☐

For Tomorrow

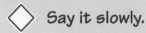 See the word.

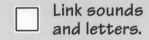 Say it slowly.

 Link sounds and letters.

 Write.

 Check.

Share What /ou/ words, spelled ou and ow, did you find?

Spelling Words	
out	now
shout	down
loud	town
mouth	brown
how	our

Name...

Kate's New Shoes

Write a spelling word to finish each sentence.

shoes   **grew**   **school**   **use**

Summer was almost here, and __(1)__ was almost over. During the year, Kate's feet __(2)__ a lot. Now she could __(3)__ a new pair of __(4)__ .

huge   **few**   **took**

Kate's mom __(5)__ her shopping. Kate tried on a __(6)__ pairs of shoes. She didn't like any of them.

"What will I do now?" asked Kate. "My feet are __(7)__ , and my left foot hurts."

room   **blue**   **look**

Then Kate tried on some __(8)__ shoes. "These shoes __(9)__ great," said Kate.

Happy ending? Not quite! That night Kate's puppy got into her __(10)__ . He chewed her new blue shoes.

1. _____
2. _____
3. _____
4. _____
5. _____
6. _____
7. _____
8. _____
9. _____
10. _____

Opposites

Opposites such as **yes** and **no** mean very different things.
Write the spelling word that is the opposite of each word below.

true
soon
loud
out
good
down
stood

1. up ➡ _____

5. in ➡ _____

2. quiet ➡ _____

6. later ➡ _____

3. false ➡ _____

7. sat ➡ _____

4. bad ➡ _____

Time to Rhyme ....

Write a word to finish each line of the rhyme.

drew   chew

8. Each day the man painted and _____,

9. Stopping only to drink and _____.

Word Ladder...........................

Go from **few** to **now** in
two steps. Change only
one letter at a time.

10. few

11. _____

12. _____

Name . . . .

blue	too
huge	two
shoes	room
new	soon
look	school
good	now

What's It All About?

Read what the story is about. Use spelling words to write a title for each story.

1. a basketball player who buys big shoes

_____

_____

2. a child's new school shoes

_____

_____

3. someone who has lots of shoes

_____

_____

4. shoes that do funny things

_____

_____

Look at the words you spelled wrong on your Unit 5 Post-Tests. Use them to write another title for a story.

_____

_____

5. _____

Proofread your sentences. Make sure your spelling, capitalization, and end marks are correct.

PROOFREADING MARKS

∧   Add
◯   Check spelling
℮   Take out
≡   Capital letter

Write All About It . . . .

Write a sentence about some funny shoes.

_____

_____

6. _____

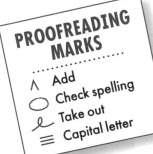

Name ....

Words That Sound the Same

Finish each sentence. Write the spelling word that sounds the same as the underlined word.

two would too our new blue

Chandra Says...

Words that sound alike can be a real problem. A wrong word that's spelled correctly is still wrong! In a story, I wrote, "The sky is blew." **Blew** is a real word, but I should have written **b-l-u-e**. Guess I blew it!

1. _____ Rover like a house made of <u>wood</u>?

2. _____ plane was an <u>hour</u> late.

3. <u>Two</u> hours is _____ long to sit.

4. I <u>knew</u> Spot would chew on my _____ shoes.

Spelling Matters!

5. I have _____ stories <u>to</u> tell you.

6. The _____ hat <u>blew</u> away.

Spelling Words

Monday	Sunday
Tuesday	week
Thursday	weekday
Friday	weekend
Saturday	Wednesday

LOOKOUT WORD

Review	Challenge
our	holiday
yellow	daily
day	

My Words

Days of the Week

A **See and Say**   Monday   Fri day
Tues day   Satur day

The names of the days of the week end with -day.

B **Link Sounds and Letters**
Sort the spelling words. Write them on the lines.

Memory Jogger

Saturday, **you are** my favourite day!

Words That Begin With Capital Letters

1. _____
2. _____
3. _____
4. _____
5. _____
6. _____
7. _____

Words That Begin With week

8. _____ 9. _____ 10. _____

C **Write and Check**
Read the riddle. Write the spelling words.

11. _____   12. _____

Riddle
Which part of the week do mice like best?

The squ-week-end!

Name . . . .

A Word Families
Circle the group of words that goes with each picture.

car, van, bike

fork, spoon, cup

coat, hat, gloves

cat, fish, bird

_____

_____

1. Seven spelling words are days of the _____ .

Write the spelling words that are days of the week.
They always begin with capital letters.

2. _____   6. _____

3. _____   7. _____

4. _____   8. _____

5. _____

B Join Two Words
Start with **week**. Then add words from
the box to write two spelling words.

| day   book   end   fall |

_____   _____

9. week + ? = _____   10. week + ? = _____

SPELL CHAT

Tell a friend about
your favourite day of the
week. Use two or more
spelling words.

Spelling Words	
Monday	Sunday
Tuesday	week
Thursday	weekday
Friday	weekend
Saturday	Wednesday

Spelling Words

Monday	Sunday
Tuesday	week
Thursday	weekday
Friday	weekend
Saturday	Wednesday

Review	Challenge
our	holiday
yellow	daily
day	

My Words

_____

_____

_____

_____

Quick Write

Write about how you helped out this weekend. Use two or more spelling words.

Ⓐ Write About a Special Person

Write about a person who likes to help others. Use two or more spelling words.

 You may do this activity on a computer.

_____

_____

_____

_____

Ⓑ Proofread

Nina wrote about her friend Ray. She found two mistakes. Find four more mistakes that Nina made, and fix them.

Tip
Write initials and special names with capital letters.

Ray p. brown lives on Main Street. He

is 15 years old. He cuts or grass every
weekend

(weeked). He takes me to soccer games

every Wensday and Saterday .

by Nina

Now proofread your sentences. Check your spelling. Make sure you put capital letters where they are needed.

PROOFREADING MARKS
∧ Add
◯ Check spelling
ℒ Take out
≡ Capital letter

Name . . . .

Ⓐ Use the Dictionary: Word History

A word history can tell how a word started.
Read the word history for **Monday**.

Monday *noun*
The second day of the week, after Sunday and before Tuesday.

Word History
In a story long ago, the moon was the wife of the sun. Since the sun had his day of the week, Sunday, the moon got her own day, too. Over time, "Moon day" became **Monday**.

1. Whose day is Monday? The _____'s day.

Ⓑ Test Yourself

Fill in the missing letters to make a spelling word.

2. W _____

3. S _____

4. M _____

5. T _ e _____

6. F _____

7. T _____ s _____

8. W _____ d

9. S _ t _____

10. W _____ s _____

11. W _____ y

Get Word Wise

The day **Saturday** was named for **Saturn**. Saturn was the Roman god of farming.

For Tomorrow

➡ See the word.

◇ Say it slowly.

☐ Link sounds and letters.

▽ Write.

⬡ Check.

Share Tell where you found the names of the days of the week. Then name the days.

Spelling Words	
Monday	Sunday
Tuesday	week
Thursday	weekday
Friday	weekend
Saturday	Wednesday

LESSON
32

Spelling Words

upon	everyone
into	anyone
inside	anyway
outside	sometimes
without	always (LOOKOUT WORD)

Review	Challenge
Wednesday	summertime
true	wintertime
way	

My Words

Learn and Spell

Name ....

Compound Words

Always has one l.
One l always
runs away!

Memory Jogger

A See and Say out+side→outside

every+one→everyone

These words are compound words. A compound word is made up of two smaller words.

B Link Sounds and Letters

Sort the spelling words. Write them on the lines.

Words With in

1. ____________________
2. ____________________

Words With out

3. ____________________
4. ____________________

Words With any

5. ____________________
6. ____________________

Word With up

7. ____________________

Word With some

8. ____________________

Word With ways

9. ____________________

Word With every

10. ____________________

C Write and Check

Read the riddle. Write the two spelling words.

11. ____________________ 12. ____________________

Riddle

Which side of a ladybug always has spots?

the outside

Vocabulary Practice Name ....

A Change a Word

Change the underlined word to make a
spelling word. Write each word once.

1. high<u>way</u> _____

2. som<u>e</u>one _____

3. up<u>set</u> _____

4. some<u>day</u> _____

5. a<u>lmost</u> _____

6. any<u>time</u> _____

7. <u>on</u>to _____

8. in<u>doors</u> _____

9. with<u>in</u> _____

10. out<u>grow</u> _____

B Make Compound Words

Draw a line from each word on the left to a word on
the right. Write the compound words.

_____

11. snow   flake   _____

12. news   ground   _____

13. play   paper   _____

Be a Spelling Sleuth
Look in a story for three
compound words such as
everyone and **anyway**.

SPELL CHAT

With a friend,
take a spelling word
apart. Try to make new
compound words with
the smaller words.

Spelling Words	
upon	everyone
into	anyone
inside	anyway
outside	sometimes
without	always

Spelling Words

upon	everyone
into	anyone
inside	anyway
outside	sometimes
without	always

Review	Challenge
Wednesday	summertime
true	wintertime
way	

My Words

Quick Write

Write about what you like to do outside. Use two or more spelling words.

Name ....

A Write About a Place

Write three or four sentences about a place you have always wanted to visit. Use two or more spelling words.

 You may do this activity on a computer.

B Proofread

Paul wrote about a place he wants to visit. He found two mistakes. Find four more mistakes that Paul made, and fix them.

Sometimes
~~Sometims~~ I dream about going to the
beach. I dig wa down ento the sand. My
                                    play
dog also dig in the sand. We ~~plays~~ and
allways have a good time.
                          by Paul

Tip
Add **s** to an action word that tells about one person, place, or thing. Do not add **s** if the action word tells about more than one.
He **talks**. They **talk**.

Now proofread your sentences. Check your spelling. Make sure you used action words correctly.

PROOFREADING MARKS
∧ Add
◯ Check spelling
ℓ Take out
≡ Capital letter

Name . . . .

Ⓐ Use the Dictionary: Definition

A definition tells the meaning of a word. Write the spelling word that goes with each definition.

The inner part of something.

1. _____

Now and then; at some times but not at others.

2. _____

Not having.

3. _____

Ⓑ Test Yourself

Write letters in the shapes to make a spelling word.

4.

5.

6.

7.

8.

9.

10.

11.

12.

13.

Get Word Wise

No one isn't written together as one word. Can you tell why?

For Tomorrow

➡️ See the word.

◇ Say it slowly.

▢ Link sounds and letters.

▽ Write.

⬡ Check.

Share What compound words did you find?

Spelling Words	
upon	everyone
into	anyone
inside	anyway
outside	sometimes
without	always

Name . . . .

Words With wh

Spelling Words

what	wheel
when	whole
where	while
who	white
whale	whose

LOOKOUT WORD

Review	Challenge
always	whisper
new	whistle
why	

My Words

A **See and Say** wh at   wh o   wh eel   wh ole

The letters **wh** stand for the beginning sound you hear in **what** and **who**.

W and **h** are quite a pair, **wh**en asking **wh**at, **wh**y, **wh**en, and **wh**ere.

Memory Jogger

B **Link Sounds and Letters**
Sort the spelling words. Write them on the lines.

Words That Begin Like **Whom**

1. _____

2. _____

3. _____

Words That Begin Like **Why**

4. _____

5. _____

6. _____

7. _____

8. _____

9. _____

10. _____

C **Write and Check**
Read the button. Write the two spelling words that begin with **wh**.

11. _____   12. _____

Say this five times fast! Which wet white whale will win?

A Question Words

Write a spelling word to finish each question.

1. _____ are you going now?

2. _____ knows the answer?

3. _____ does school begin?

4. _____ is your name?

5. _____ hair is red?

B Word Clues

Write a spelling word for each clue.

6. I sound just like **hole**. _____

7. I rhyme with **smile**. _____

8. I swim in the sea. _____

9. I am a colour. _____

10. I can roll. _____

Be a Spelling Sleuth

Look in newspapers for three words that begin with wh, such as **when** and **what**.

SPELL CHAT

Ask a friend a question. Start with **what, when, where,** or **who**. See if your friend can answer with a spelling word.

Spelling Words	
what	wheel
when	whole
where	while
who	white
whale	whose

Spelling Words

what	wheel
when	whole
where	while
who	white
whale	whose

Review	Challenge
always	whisper
new	whistle
why	

My Words

Quick Write

Your friend came back from a trip. Write two questions you will ask. Use two or more spelling words.

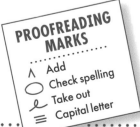

A **Write a Poem**
Write spelling words to finish this poem.

Goat Fun

Mom took me to Parker Farm,
___1___ I saw a small ___2___ goat.

I fed him and he sniffed my arm.
___3___ fun to pet his coat!

B **Proofread**
Mei wrote this poem about a family trip. She found two mistakes. Find four more mistakes that Mei made, and fix them.

Mei

At sea Park
What
(Whot) did we see at Sea park?

We saw a wale and a wite shark.

We saw a seal all shiny and dark.

He allways rolled over to bark!

You may do this activity on a computer.

1. _____

2. _____

3. _____

Tip
Remember to write the name of a special place with a capital letter.

PROOFREADING MARKS

∧ Add
◯ Check spelling
ℓ Take out
≡ Capital letter

Proofread the poem you finished. Check your spelling. Make sure you put capital letters where they are needed.

A Use the Dictionary: Definitions

Some words have more than one meaning. Read the two meanings for **white**. Write the number of the definition that matches each underlined word.

> **white**
> 1. *noun* The lightest colour; the colour of snow or milk.
> 2. *noun* The **white** of an egg is the part around the yolk.

1. _____ Dad used an egg <u>white</u> to make pancakes.

2. _____ My favourite colour is <u>white</u>.

B Test Yourself

Solve each word puzzle to write a spelling word.

3. wh + feel - f = _____

4. wh + bite - b = _____

5. wh + ten - t = _____

6. why - y + o = _____

7. wh + sale - s = _____

8. wh + those - th = _____

9. wh + pole - p = _____

10. wham - m + t = _____

11. wh + smile - sm = _____

12. wh + there - th = _____

Get Word Wise

A whale is a large animal. Sometimes we use **whale** to tell about something big. Here's one example: "That's a **whale** of an idea."

For Tomorrow

 See the word.

◇ Say it slowly.

☐ Link sounds and letters.

▽ Write.

⬟ Check.

Share What words with **wh** did you find?

Spelling Words	
what	wheel
when	whole
where	while
who	white
whale	whose

Name ....

LESSON 34

Spelling Words

bees	dishes
skates	wishes
twins	lunches
boxes	branches
foxes	places LOOKOUT WORD

Review	Challenge
whose	sandwiches
book	tomatoes
tree	

My Words

Plurals

Listen, my friend! Add **es** if **sh**, **ch**, or **x** is at the end!

A **See and Say**   skate(s)   fox(es)
twin(s)   dish(es)

These words are plurals. Plurals are words that name more than one thing. Some plurals end in s. Some end in es.

B **Link Sounds and Letters**
Sort the spelling words. Write them on the lines.

Memory Jogger

+ s
1. _____
2. _____
3. _____
4. _____

x + es
5. _____
6. _____

sh + es
7. _____
8. _____

ch + es
9. _____
10. _____

C **Write and Check**
Find three plurals in the riddle.
Write the two spelling words.

11. _____   12. _____

Riddle
How do bees go places?

in buzzes

Name ....

Ⓐ Plurals With s

Add **s** to most naming words to tell about more than one. Use each picture clue to write a spelling word that names more than one.

1. _____

2. _____

3. _____

4. _____

Ⓑ Plurals With es

Add **es** to naming words that end in **x**, **sh**, or **ch** to tell about more than one. Write a spelling word to finish each phrase.

_____

5. one lunch, many _____

6. a branch, a few _____

7. that box, those _____

8. a fox, some _____

9. one wish, three _____

10. one dish, two _____

Be a Spelling Sleuth

Look on labels for three plurals such as **skates** and **dishes**.

SPELL CHAT

Share two wishes with a classmate. Use two or more spelling words.

Spelling Words	
bees	dishes
skates	wishes
twins	lunches
boxes	branches
foxes	places

Name . . . .

Spelling Words

bees	dishes
skates	wishes
twins	lunches
boxes	branches
foxes	places

Review	Challenge
whose	sandwiches
book	tomatoes
tree	

My Words

Quick Write

What job would you like someday? Write about it, using two spelling words.

Ⓐ Write a Help-Wanted Sign

Pine Park needs a young helper for the park ranger. Write a help-wanted sign for the job. Use two or more spelling words.

 You may do this activity on a computer.

Ⓑ Proofread

Otto wrote this help-wanted sign. He found two mistakes. Find four more mistakes that Otto made, and fix them.

> **Tip**
> Remember that a telling sentence ends with a period and a question ends with a question mark.

Do you wish to spend time in plases outside

Are you someone (whoz) weekends are free ?
whose

Pine Park needs a helper for the park ranger

You will help feed the foxs .

You will also cut tree branchs on the paths.

Proofread your sign. Check your spelling. Be sure you used the correct end marks.

PROOFREADING MARKS

ʌ Add
◯ Check spelling
ℓ Take out
≡ Capital letter

ⓐ Use the Dictionary: Word Endings

A word can have one or more different endings. The new words are in dark type at the end of the entry.

> **wish**
> 1. *noun* A strong desire or longing for something.
> 2. *verb* To want something very much. *I wish I could go home now.*
> 3. *verb* To hope for something for somebody else. *I wish you a happy new year!* ▷ *verb* **wishes, wishing, wished**

Write **wish** with three different endings.

1. _____ _____ _____

ⓑ Test Yourself

Write each spelling word with **s** or **es**. Circle the plural words that have two syllables.

2. twin _____

3. box _____

4. bee _____

5. lunch _____

6. dish _____

7. branch _____

8. skate _____

9. fox _____

10. place _____

11. wish _____

Spelling Words

foot	mice
feet	man
tooth	men
teeth	woman
mouse	women

Review	Challenge
places	goose
school	geese
team	

My Words

Unusual Plurals

A See and Say

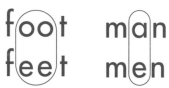

foot   man
feet   men

Most of the time you add **s** or **es** to a naming word to form the plural. Sometimes you have to change the spelling of the word.

B Link Sounds and Letters

Sort the spelling words by the way they become plurals. Write the word that names **one** first.

oo → ee

1. _____
2. _____
3. _____
4. _____

ouse → ice

5. _____
6. _____

a → e

7. _____
8. _____
9. _____
10. _____

C Write and Check

Write the plural spelling word in the riddle.

_____

11. _____

*The word **tooth** has an **o** and another **o, too.***

Memory Jogger

LOOKOUT WORD

Riddle
What has lots of teeth but no mouth?

a comb

A Make New Words

Add and take away letters to write spelling words.

1. m + fan - f = _____

2. tool - l + th = _____

3. m + nice - n = _____

4. met - t + n = _____

5. m + house - h = _____

6. word + man - rd = _____

7. w + come - c + n = _____

8. fork - rk + ot = _____

B One and More Than One

Write a spelling word to finish the phrase that describes each picture.

9. left _____

10. both _____

11.  one _____

12. many _____

13. two _____

14. a _____

Be a Spelling Sleuth

Look in magazines for two unusual plurals such as **men** and **women**.

SPELL CHAT

Use a spelling word that means "**one**" in a sentence. Your partner uses the plural of that word.

Spelling Words	
foot	mice
feet	man
tooth	men
teeth	woman
mouse	women

Spelling Words

foot	mice
feet	man
tooth	men
teeth	woman
mouse	women

Review	Challenge
places	goose
school	geese
team	

My Words

Quick Write

Write about a special place you have visited. Use two or more spelling words.

A Write a Message

Write a message to a friend. Tell about a walk you took. Use two or more spelling words.

 You may do this activity on a computer.

B Proofread

Dan wrote a message. He found three mistakes. Find four more mistakes that Dan made, and fix them.

Tip
Always use commas between words in a list.

To Kip,

                                    school
Meet me for a hike after (skool).

I went the other day and saw geese, birds,

and mouses with little teath.

I saw two womin pick flowers.

I walked so long that my fet still hurt!

                      From Dan

PROOFREADING MARKS

∧ Add

◯ Check spelling

ℓ Take out

≡ Capital letter

Now proofread your message. Check your spelling. Make sure you use commas where they are needed.

A Use the Dictionary: Example Sentences

An example sentence in a dictionary can show you how to use a word. Read the meanings in this entry. Circle the example sentence.

foot   *noun*
1. Part of your body at the end of your leg.
2. The bottom or lower end of something.
3. If you **put your foot down,** you insist on something and act firmly.
Mom put her foot down about my going to bed on time.

Write a sentence for one of the other meanings of **foot**.

1. _____

B Test Yourself

Use the secret code to write the spelling words.

 a   e   f   h   i   m   n   o   s   t   u   w

2. _____

3. _____

4. _____

5. _____

6. _____

7. _____

8. _____

9. _____

10. _____

11. _____

Get Word Wise

A **mouse** is fast and quiet. Its tail is long. How do you think a computer **mouse** got its name?

For Tomorrow

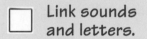 See the word.

◇ Say it slowly.

□ Link sounds and letters.

▽ Write.

⬡ Check.

Share What unusual plurals did you find?

Spelling Words	
foot	mice
feet	man
tooth	men
teeth	woman
mouse	women

Name . . . .

This Is Really the End!

Write a spelling word to finish each sentence.

anyway   when   Monday

Our last week of school was very busy. We did something special every day. On __(1)__, we went to the playground. It was cool, but we went out __(2)__. __(3)__ it began to rain, we went inside.

Tuesday   places   Wednesday

On __(4)__, we visited two different __(5)__. First we went to the park. Then we went on a boat.

On __(6)__, we made a picture book about our trip.

Thursday   where   Friday   wishes

On __(7)__, our teacher asked us __(8)__ we want to go for summer vacation.

On __(9)__, we made __(10)__ for next year. I wished for a good year in school.

1.
2.
3.
4.
5.
6.
7.
8.
9.
10.

Name ....

Opposites

Opposites such as **in** and **out** mean very different things.
Write the opposite of each word.

1. man _____

2. outside _____   4. never _____

3. no one _____   5. inside _____

outside

woman

everyone

always

inside

Sayings...

Write a word to finish each saying.

6. A short time is "just a little _____."

7. If you like sweet foods, you have a "sweet _____."

8. When you are afraid to do something, you have "cold _____."

feet

while

tooth

Letter Change...

Change the underlined letter in each word.
Make a spelling word.

9. wh<u>y</u> _____   10. <u>c</u>hat _____

who

what

Friday   when
inside   where
outside   who
everyone   twins
always   boxes
what   lunches

Proofread your questions. Make sure your spelling, capitalization, and end marks are correct.

PROOFREADING MARKS

∧ Add
◯ Check spelling
ℓ Take out
≡ Capital letter

Name ....

Answers and Questions

Read each answer. Write a question to go with it.
Use one or two spelling words in the question.

1. Jeff and Josh are Ellen's twin brothers.

_____

- -

_____

2. Jeff and Josh hid in the bushes when they heard Ellen.

_____

- -

_____

3. Then they found kittens in some boxes.

_____

- -

_____

4. Soon it will be time to eat.

_____

- -

_____

Look at the words you spelled wrong on your Unit 6 Post-Tests.
Use them to write another question.

5. _____

Do You Ever Wonder? ....

Write a question you have about a favourite story.

_____

- -

6. _____

Tip
Remember that a question ends with a question mark.

Name ....

More Than One

Read each pair of sentences. Write a word to finish the second sentence. Use the underlined word as a clue.

1. Jill is missing a front <u>tooth</u>.

   _____

   Ben has lost both front _____.

2. The teacher is a <u>woman</u>.

   _____

   All the students are _____.

3. Which <u>box</u> has cat food?

   _____

   All of the _____ are shut.

4. I can't find my <u>lunch</u>.

   _____

   Did Dan forget to pack the _____?

5. Can you tell which <u>twin</u> is Anita?

   _____

   Those _____ look so much alike!

lunches
teeth
twins
women
boxes

Spelling Matters!

Nick Says...

You add **s** to make most words name more than one, but not always. In a story about a friendly elf, I wrote "The elf gave me three **wishs**." My teacher put my story on the wall— wrong spelling and all! Now if I had three **wishes**, I would fix that mistake.

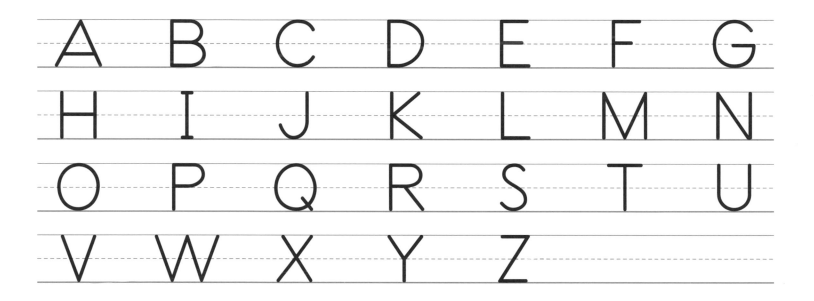

A B C D E F G
H I J K L M N
O P Q R S T U
V W X Y Z

a b c d e f g h i j
k l m n o p q r s t
u v w x y z

afraid	from	most	put	that	went
always	gone	mother	right	them	what
am	good	much	roll	then	when
anyone	has	name	said	there	where
anyway	have	new	Saturday	these	which
as	hello	nice	school	think	while
blue	high	none	send	this	white
come	him	now	shoes	time	who
could	how	off	should	today	whole
does	if	on	show	too	whose
done	inside	once	some	two	with
down	into	one	sometimes	upon	woman
easy	live	our	soon	use	women
eight	love	out	Sunday	very	would
every	many	outside	sure	was	write
everyone	might	play	talk	Wednesday	
father	money	pretty	than	well	

You will find all your spelling words in ABC order in the Spelling Dictionary. This page shows you how to use it.

This is the word you look up. It is the **entry word.**

This is the **sentence** that uses the entry word. It helps you know what the word means.

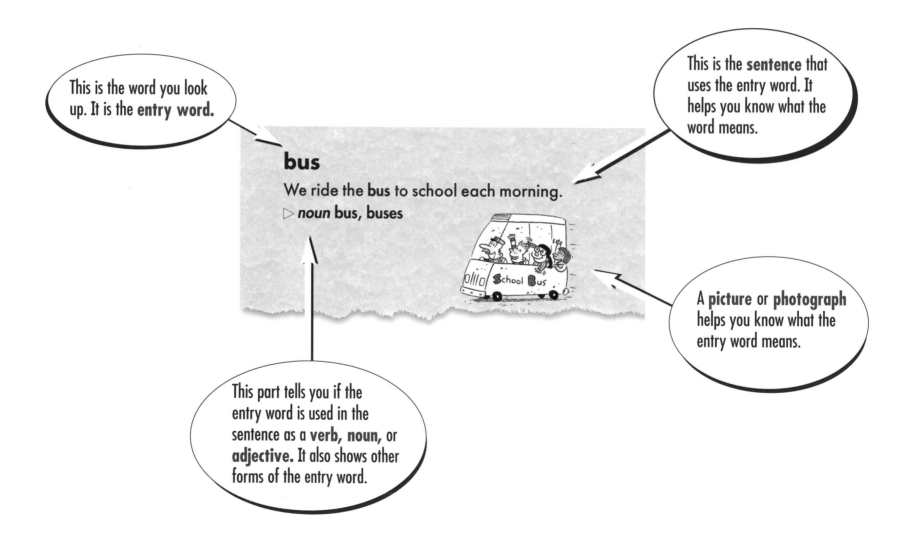

bus

We ride the **bus** to school each morning.
▷ *noun* bus, buses

A **picture** or **photograph** helps you know what the entry word means.

This part tells you if the entry word is used in the sentence as a **verb, noun,** or **adjective.** It also shows other forms of the entry word.

Aa

above

The sun and clouds are **above** us.
Opposite **below**

ache

I fell, and now my legs **ache**.
▶ *verb* **ache, aching, ached**

act

She wants to **act** in a play.
▶ *verb* **act, acting, acted**

add

We **add** sugar to lemonade to make it sweet. ▶ *verb* **add, adding, added**

afraid

The young child is **afraid** of the dark.
▶ *adjective*

agree

Mom and I **agree** that it's time for bed. ▶ *verb* **agree, agreeing, agreed**

all

I put **all** of my toys away after playing with them.
Opposite **none**

always

He will **always** be my brother.

am

Do you know who I **am**? I **am** your new teacher. ▶ *verb* **be, am, is, are, being, was, were, been**

any

I don't have **any** crayons at all.
▶ *adjective*

Spelling Dictionary

anyone
Anyone who wants to can come to the picnic.

anyway
I can't go to the party. I don't want to **anyway**.

as
I am **as** hungry **as** a horse!

ask
You can **ask** for help if you need to.
▶ *verb* **ask, asking, asked**

away
The cat ran **away** from the dog.

Bb

ball
Throw the **ball**! ▶ *noun* **ball, balls**

bath
I washed myself when I took a **bath**.
▶ *noun* **bath, baths**

bathroom
She is brushing her teeth in the **bathroom**.
▶ *noun* **bathroom, bathrooms**

beanstalk
There is a **beanstalk** in my garden.
▶ *noun* **beanstalk, beanstalks**

beat
I like to **beat** the drum.
▶ *verb* **beat, beating, beat, beaten**

bees
Bees fly from flower to flower.
▶ *noun* **bee, bees**

best
This is the **best** way to go.
▶ *adjective* **good, better, best**

blame

Don't **blame** me! I didn't make that mess!
▶ *verb* **blame, blaming, blamed**

blew

The wind **blew** the papers off the desk.
▶ *verb* **blow, blowing, blew, blown**

blow

He will **blow** the whistle to make them stop.
▶ *verb* **blow, blowing, blew, blown**

blue

The sky is **blue**.
▶ *adjective*

boat

We took a **boat** out to sea. ▶ *noun* **boat, boats**

bold

The **bold** girl was not afraid of the dog.
▶ *adjective* **bold, bolder, boldest**

book

She read a **book** about sea lions.
▶ *noun* **book, books**

boot

My **boot** is on my foot. ▶ *noun* **boot, boots**

both

I like **both** of the stories I read last week.
▶ *adjective*

box

There are old dishes in this **box**.
▶ *noun* **box, boxes**

boxes

We packed everything in **boxes** when we moved.
▶ *noun* **box, boxes**

branch

A **branch** broke and fell off the tree.
▶ *noun* **branch, branches**

branches

The **branches** have no leaves in winter.
▶ *noun* **branch, branches**

brave

A **brave** boy climbed up the tree to get the cat.
▶ *adjective* **brave, braver, bravest**

bright

The stars look **bright** in the dark sky.
▶ *adjective* **bright, brighter, brightest**

broom

Use the **broom** to sweep up the dust.
▶ *noun* **broom, brooms**

brown

Brown is a colour. Mud is **brown**. ▶ *adjective*

bump

The car hit a **bump** in the road.
▶ *noun* **bump, bumps**

bunch

For a snack we ate a **bunch** of grapes.
▶ *noun* **bunch, bunches**

bus

We ride the **bus** to school each morning.
▶ *noun* **bus, buses**

Cc

call

I will **call** my mom on the phone.
▶ *verb* **call, calling, called**

camp

I spent two weeks at summer **camp**.
▶ *noun* **camp, camps**

chalkboard

My teacher wrote a sentence on the **chalkboard**.
▶ *noun* **chalkboard, chalkboards**

chase

My dog likes to **chase** cats.
▶ *verb* **chase, chasing, chased**

cheetah

A **cheetah** is a very fast animal.
It is part of the cat family.
▶ *noun* **cheetah, cheetahs**

chew

It is important to **chew** your food well.
▶ *verb* **chew, chewing, chewed**

children

All the **children** in my class saw the puppet show.
▶ *noun* **child, children**

chip

A **chip** came off the mug when it fell. The mug fell on the floor.
Now there is a **chip** in it.
▶ *noun* **chip, chips**

chop

Dad used an axe to **chop** the wood.
▶ *verb* **chop, chopping, chopped**

coat

I wear a **coat** when it is cold. ▶ *noun* **coat, coats**

cold

It feels very **cold** outside in the snow.
▶ *adjective* **cold, colder, coldest**

come

Can you **come** home with me? Yes, I can **come**.
▶ *verb* **come, coming, came, come**

cook

Dad will **cook** dinner for us.
▶ *verb* **cook, cooking, cooked**

could

I **could** not reach the top shelf. ▶ *verb* **can, could**

creature

Never hurt any living **creature**.
▶ *noun* **creature, creatures**

crocodile

The **crocodile** lives in the swamp.
▶ *noun* **crocodile, crocodiles**

cruel
It is **cruel** not to feed a hungry pet.
▶ *adjective* **cruel, crueler, cruelest**

cute
That bow in your hair looks **cute**.
▶ *adjective* **cute, cuter, cutest**

daily
My family reads a **daily** newspaper. ▶ *adjective*

dew
The grass is wet with **dew**. ▶ *noun*

dish
Put the food in a clean **dish**. ▶ *noun* **dish, dishes**

dishes
I washed the dirty **dishes** after dinner.
▶ *noun* **dish, dishes**

does
Does the bus stop here? Yes, it **does**.
▶ *verb* **do, does, doing, did, done**

done
He did the work. Now the work is **done**.
▶ *verb* **do, does, doing, did, done**

down
A tree fell **down** in the storm.
Opposite **up**

dream
We **dream** when we are asleep.
What did you **dream** about last night?
▶ *verb* **dream, dreaming, dreamed**

drew
The girl **drew** a picture of a train.
▶ *verb* **draw, drawing, drew, drawn**

duck
We feed bread to the **duck**. ▶ *noun* **duck, ducks**

each
There are five apples and five children. **Each** child gets one apple. ▶ *adjective*

easy
I can do all the math problems. They are **easy**!
▶ *adjective* **easy, easier, easiest**

eight
Eight is the number after seven. ▶ *noun*

end
Did you finish the book? How does it **end**? ▶ *verb* **end, ending, ended**

every
Every boy here is wearing sneakers.
▶ *adjective*

everyone
Everyone needs clean air to breathe.
Opposite **no one**

face
My baby sister fed herself. Now she has food all over her **face**. ▶ *noun* **face, faces**

fall
Look outside. You can see the rain **fall**.
▶ *verb* **fall, falling, fell, fallen**

fantasy
My **fantasy** is to meet a real live dinosaur.
▶ *noun* **fantasy, fantasies**

fast
She is a **fast** runner.
▶ *adjective* **fast, faster, fastest**

father
I look just like my **father**! ▶ *noun* **father, fathers**

feel
How do you **feel** this morning? I **feel** good.
▶ *verb* **feel, feeling, felt**

feet
I walked so far my **feet** hurt.
▶ *noun* **foot, feet**

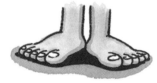

few

I picked a **few** flowers. I wish I had more.
▶ *adjective* **few, fewer, fewest**

fight

The puppies got into a **fight** over a bone.
▶ *noun* **fight, fights**

fine

It is a **fine** day for a swim.
▶ *adjective* **fine, finer, finest**

finish

When I **finish** my work, I will go play.
▶ *verb* **finish, finishes, finishing, finished**

fish

The **fish** swam up the stream.
▶ *noun* **fish, fish** or **fishes**

fix

My mom can **fix** anything that is broken.
▶ *verb* **fix, fixes, fixing, fixed**

flew

The bird **flew** out of the nest.
▶ *verb* **fly, flying, flew, flown**

float

Boats **float** in the water.
▶ *verb* **float, floating, floated**

fold

Fold the clothes before you put them away.
▶ *verb* **fold, folding, folded**

food

What is your favourite **food**? My favourite **food** is rice. ▶ *noun* **food, foods**

foot

My **foot** just fits into that shoe.
▶ *noun* **foot, feet**

fox

The **fox** is a wild animal. It looks like a dog. ▶ *noun* **fox, foxes**

foxes
Baby **foxes** are called kits. ▶ *noun* **fox, foxes**

Friday
Friday is the last day of school in the week.
▶ *noun* **Friday, Fridays**

from
This letter came all the way **from** Spain.

funny
I laughed at the **funny** jokes.
▶ *adjective* **funny, funnier, funniest**

geese
The **geese** flew south for the winter.
▶ *noun* **goose, geese**

gift
The boy gave his mom a **gift** for her birthday.
▶ *noun* **gift, gifts**

glue
The children used **glue** on the paper. ▶ *noun*

goat
A **goat** has horns and
some hair under its chin.
▶ *noun* **goat, goats**

gold
The leaves are red and **gold** in the fall.
▶ *adjective*

gone
Where is everyone? They have all **gone** home.
▶ *verb* **go, goes, going, went, gone**

good
I liked reading the book. It was a **good** book.
▶ *adjective* **good, better, best**

good night
Before I go to bed, I tell my mom and dad
good night.

goose

A **goose** is a bird that looks like a duck. It is bigger than a duck and has a longer neck.

▶ *noun* **goose, geese**

grass

The **grass** is still wet from the rain.

▶ *noun* **grass, grasses**

great

The boy built a **great,** big sand castle.

▶ *adjective* **great, greater, greatest**

grew

The girl **grew** two centimetres last year.

▶ *verb* **grow, growing, grew, grown**

grow

Flowers need water and sun to **grow**.

▶ *verb* **grow, growing, grew, grown**

Hh

hall

The teacher hung our art work in the **hall** so everyone could see it. ▶ *noun* **hall, halls**

hand

The child held her grandmother's **hand** while they crossed the street. ▶ *noun* **hand, hands**

happy

We were **happy** when we won the soccer game.

▶ *adjective* **happy, happier, happiest**

has

The girl **has** a red bicycle. She loves to ride it.

▶ *verb* **have, has, having, had**

have

They **have** the same backpacks.

▶ *verb* **have, has, having, had**

hello

I always say **hello** when I answer the phone. *Opposite* **goodbye**

help

Sometimes I need **help** with my spelling homework. ▶ *noun*

high

The hill is hard to climb. It is very **high**.
▶ *adjective* **high, higher, highest**

him

The boy is my friend. I like to play with **him**.
Opposite **her**

hold

I like to **hold** my baby sister on my lap.
▶ *verb* **hold, holding, held**

holiday

Canada Day is my favourite **holiday**.
▶ *noun* **holiday, holidays**

how

Do you know **how** to play checkers?

howl

Listen to the dogs **howl** at the moon!
▶ *verb* **howl, howling, howled**

huge

An elephant is a **huge** animal.
▶ *adjective* **huge, huger, hugest**

hunt

I can't find my sock. Will you help me **hunt** for it?
▶ *verb* **hunt, hunting, hunted**

Ii

if

If you want the apple, you can have it.

inside

It's raining. Let's go **inside** and get dry.
Opposite **outside**

into

He reached **into** the bag for some nuts.

Kk

koala

A **koala** looks like a small bear but is related to the kangaroo.
▶ *noun* **koala, koalas**

land

The **land** here is very hilly. ▶ *noun*

last

He was the **last** person to come to the party. *Opposite* **first**

less

The brown cat has **less** hair than the black cat. *Opposite* **more**

lesson

Today's science **lesson** was about the planets.
▶ *noun* **lesson, lessons**

lift

Can you **lift** that box onto the table?
▶ *verb* **lift, lifting, lifted**

light

Turn on the **light**. It is dark in here.
▶ *verb* **light, lighting, lit**

line

I wrote my name on the top **line** of the paper.
▶ *noun* **line, lines**

listen

If you **listen**, you can hear the birds singing.
▶ *verb* **listen, listening, listened**

little

An ant is a **little** insect.
▶ *adjective* **little, littler, littlest**

live

Where do you **live**? I **live** in Canada.
▶ *verb* **live, living, lived**

look

You can **look** in the mirror to see your face.
▶ *verb* **look, looking, looked**

lot

Squirrels put away a **lot** of nuts for the winter.
▶ *noun*

loud

The children in the class were **loud**. The teacher asked them to be quiet.
▶ *adjective* **loud, louder, loudest**

love

We **love** our dog. ▶ *verb* **love, loving, loved**

low

I could reach the book. It was on a **low** shelf.
▶ *adjective* **low, lower, lowest**

luck

She found her ring. That was good **luck**.
▶ *noun*

lunch

He had a bowl of soup for **lunch**.
▶ *noun* **lunch, lunches**

lunches

Our school serves hot **lunches** every day.
▶ *noun* **lunch, lunches**

Mm

mad

The girl got **mad** when her pen broke.
▶ *adjective* **mad, madder, maddest**

mail

We picked up our **mail** at the post office. There was a letter and a package. ▶ *noun*

man

My little brother will grow up to be a **man**.
▶ *noun* **man, men**

many

There are **many** children in our school.
Opposite **few**

men

Boys grow up to be **men**.
▸ *noun* **man, men**

mess

A raccoon knocked over the trash. What a **mess**!
▸ *noun* **mess, messes**

mice

The poem was about three **mice**.
▸ *noun* **mouse, mice**

midnight

Midnight is at twelve o'clock. ▸ *noun*

might

I **might** go skating, but I **might** not.
▸ *verb* **may, might**

milk

Pour some **milk** on your cereal. ▸ *noun*

miss

The batter wants to hit the ball. Will she **miss** it?
▸ *verb* **miss, misses, missing, missed**

mix

Mix yellow and blue paint to get green.
▸ *verb* **mix, mixes, mixing, mixed**

Monday

Monday is the first day of school in the week.
▸ *noun* **Monday, Mondays**

money

I save my **money** in a bank. ▸ *noun*

moon

I see the **moon** at night. ▸ *noun* **moon, moons**

most

Most babies sleep a lot. ▸ *adjective*

mother

My **mother** goes to work every day.
▸ *noun* **mother, mothers**

mouse
The cat chases the **mouse**. ▶ *noun* **mouse, mice**

mouth
Do not talk when your **mouth** is full.
▶ *noun* **mouth, mouths**

much
How **much** money does a newspaper cost?
▶ *adjective*

mud
When it rains, the dirt turns into **mud**. ▶ *noun*

must
Dad says I **must** do my homework every day.
▶ *verb*

mystery
Why won't the flashlight work? It is a **mystery** to me. ▶ *noun* **mystery, mysteries**

Nn

name
I wrote my **name** at the top of my paper.
▶ *noun* **name, names**

need
I **need** to wear sneakers to gym class.
▶ *verb* **need, needing, needed**

new
My **new** shoes hurt my feet.
▶ *adjective* **new, newer, newest**

newspaper
My mother reads the **newspaper** every morning.
▶ *noun* **newspaper, newspapers**

next
She took a turn jumping rope. Who is **next**?

nice
We had a **nice** time at the party.
▶ *adjective* **nice, nicer, nicest**

night
It gets dark at **night**. ▶ *noun* **night, nights**

nine
The number **nine** comes between eight and ten. ▶ *noun*

none
None of the paint is left. We used it up yesterday.
Opposite **all**

notebook
Write your homework in your school **notebook**.
▶ *noun* **notebook, notebooks**

now
Do you want to eat your lunch **now** or later?

nut
The **nut** fell from the tree.
▶ *noun* **nut, nuts**

Oo

odd
We need to fix the car. It makes an **odd** noise.
▶ *adjective* **odd, odder, oddest**

of
One **of** my pencils is broken.

off
We got **off** the bus at the park.
Opposite **on**

old
I've had this doll a long time. It is very **old**.
▶ *adjective* **old, older, oldest**

on
The plates are **on** the table.
Opposite **off**

once
I visit my grandfather **once** a week.

one
I have only **one** cracker left.
▶ *adjective*

our
Our teacher tells good stories.
Opposite **your**

out
Let's go **out** for dinner.
Opposite **in**

outside
The children played **outside** in the snow.
Opposite **inside**

own
I don't need to use your pen. I have my **own** pen.

Pp

paint
She used red **paint** to colour the truck.
▶ *noun* **paint, paints**

parachute
The pilot jumped from the plane with a **parachute**. He landed safely.
▶ *noun* **parachute, parachutes**

pay
I will **pay** for the book. ▶ *verb* **pay, paying, paid**

picnic
My family went on a **picnic** in the park. We packed sandwiches. ▶ *noun* **picnic, picnics**

place
Here is a good **place** to hang your coat.
▶ *noun* **place, places**

places
What **places** did you visit on your trip?
▶ *noun* **place, places**

play
We like to **play** tic-tac-toe.
▶ *verb* **play, playing, played**

playground

There is a great slide at our school **playground**.
▶ *noun* **playground, playgrounds**

playmate

My friend plays with me every day. He is my
playmate. ▶ *noun* **playmate, playmates**

pool

The children were swimming in a small **pool**.
▶ *noun* **pool, pools**

pretty

Those red flowers are **pretty**.
▶ *adjective* **pretty, prettier, prettiest**

puddle

After the storm there was a **puddle**
on the sidewalk. I splashed in it.
▶ *noun* **puddle, puddles**

puppy

The **puppy** will grow up to be a dog.
▶ *noun* **puppy, puppies**

push

I had to **push** my bike up the hill.
▶ *verb* **push, pushes, pushing, pushed**

put

Where did you **put** the chair? I can't find it.
▶ *verb* **put, putting, put**

Rr

rain

I got wet from walking in the **rain**. ▶ *noun*

rest

He is tired. He will need to **rest**.
▶ *verb* **rest, resting, rested**

rich

She had a lot of money. She felt **rich**.
▶ *adjective* **rich, richer, richest**

right

The school is on the **right** side of the road,
not the left side. ▶ *adjective*

road

Look out for cars before you cross the **road**.
▶ *noun* **road, roads**

rock

The **rock** is hard. ▶ *noun* **rock, rocks**

rocket

A **rocket** landed on the moon.
▶ *noun* **rocket, rockets**

roll

A ball will **roll** down a hill.
▶ *verb* **roll, rolling, rolled**

roller coaster

We rode on the **roller coaster**.
▶ *noun* **roller coaster, roller coasters**

room

This is my **room**. I sleep and play
in my **room**. ▶ *noun* **room, rooms**

rule

My dad's **rule** is that I have to make my bed.
▶ *noun* **rule, rules**

rush

We got up late. We had to **rush** to get ready.
▶ *verb* **rush, rushes, rushing, rushed**

Ss

said

My brother **said** that I was a good skater.
▶ *verb* **say, says, saying, said**

same

My sister and I like the **same** sports. We both
swim and play ball. ▶ *adjective*

sandwiches

We bought bread and ham to make some
sandwiches. ▶ *noun* **sandwich, sandwiches**

Saturday

I wake up late every **Saturday** morning.
▶ *noun* **Saturday, Saturdays**

save

I want to **save** enough money to buy a bike.
▶ *verb* **save, saving, saved**

school

Dad drives me to **school** because he teaches there. ▶ *noun* **school, schools**

schoolyard

We play ball in the **schoolyard**.
▶ *noun* **schoolyard, schoolyards**

scold

I **scold** my dog when he eats my food.
▶ *verb* **scold, scolding, scolded**

send

I will **send** my grandmother a letter.
▶ *verb* **send, sending, sent**

sew

Use this needle and some thread to **sew** on the button. ▶ *verb* **sew, sewing, sewed, sewn**

shadow

I can see my **shadow**.
▶ *noun* **shadow, shadows**

shall

I **shall** eat pancakes for breakfast.
▶ *verb* **shall, should**

shape

A circle is a **shape**. So is a square.
▶ *noun* **shape, shapes**

sheep

I saw a **sheep** on the farm.
▶ *noun* **sheep, sheep**

shell

A turtle's **shell** is hard. ▶ *noun* **shell, shells**

ship
The **ship** sailed across the ocean.
- ▸ *noun* **ship, ships**

shoes
First I put on my socks. Then I put on my **shoes**.
- ▸ *noun* **shoe, shoes**

shop
This new **shop** has toys for sale.
- ▸ *noun* **shop, shops**

should
I **should** do my homework before dinner.
- ▸ *verb* **shall, should**

shout
Please don't **shout**. I can hear you.
- ▸ *verb* **shout, shouting, shouted**

show
Can you **show** me where the town is on a map?
- ▸ *verb* **show, showing, showed**

shut
The door is open. Can you **shut** it?
- ▸ *verb* **shut, shutting, shut**

side
The bookstore is on the other **side** of the street.
- ▸ *noun* **side, sides**

sidewalk
Walk on the **sidewalk**, not on the road.
- ▸ *noun* **sidewalk, sidewalks**

sight
The boy hid behind a bush. He was out of **sight**.
- ▸ *noun* **sight, sights**

six
I was **six** years old in first grade.

skate
This **skate** fits very well.
- ▸ *noun* **skate, skates**

Spelling Dictionary

skates
My **skates** glide smoothly over the ice.
▶ *noun* **skate, skates**

slide
I like to **slide** down the hill on my sled.
▶ *verb* **slide, slides, sliding, slid**

smile
When I am happy, I **smile**.
▶ *verb* **smile, smiling, smiled**

snail
I saw a **snail** at the beach.
▶ *noun* **snail, snails**

snake
A **snake** is a long, thin animal. It has no legs. ▶ *noun* **snake, snakes**

snow
We put on warm clothes so we could play outside in the **snow**. ▶ *noun*

snowflake
A **snowflake** is a little piece of snow.
▶ *noun* **snowflake, snowflakes**

soak
A towel will **soak** up the water on the floor.
▶ *verb* **soak, soaking, soaked**

soap
Use **soap** and hot water to wash your hands.
▶ *noun*

socks
My **socks** keep my feet warm.
▶ *noun* **sock, socks**

sold
The woman **sold** me a hat for two dollars.
▶ *verb* **sell, selling, sold**

some
I would like to eat **some** fruit. ▶ *adjective*

sometimes
Sometimes I like to take a nap but not always.

soon

I am very hungry. I hope we eat **soon**.

sorry

I am **sorry** that you are sick. I hope you feel better soon. ▶ *adjective* **sorry, sorrier, sorriest**

spend

I can **spend** one dollar at the fair.
▶ *verb* **spend, spending, spent**

spot

The ink made a **spot** on the shirt.
▶ *noun* **spot, spots**

spotted

The dog is **spotted**. ▶ *adjective*

stamp

Put a **stamp** on the letter before you mail it.
▶ *noun* **stamp, stamps**

stand

We **stand** in line to get our lunch.
▶ *verb* **stand, standing, stood**

stick

I found a **stick** under the old tree.
▶ *noun* **stick, sticks**

stomach

I just ate. My **stomach** is full.
▶ *noun* **stomach, stomachs**

stone

The **stone** in my shoe hurts my foot.
▶ *noun* **stone, stones**

stood

She **stood** on the stool to reach the high shelf.
▶ *verb* **stand, standing, stood**

stop

All cars must **stop** at red lights.
▶ *verb* **stop, stopping, stopped**

Spelling Dictionary

story

I love it when Grandpa tells me a **story**.
▶ *noun* **story, stories**

street

My school is on this **street**. ▶ *noun* **street, streets**

stroll

Take a **stroll** with me. It's a nice day for a walk.
▶ *noun* **stroll, strolls**

student

I am a **student** at Park Street School.
▶ *noun* **student, students**

such

I have never read **such** a great book before.
▶ *adjective*

summertime

I play outside in **summertime**.
My friends and I like the
warm weather. ▶ *noun*

Sunday

Sunday is my favourite day of the week.
▶ *noun* **Sunday, Sundays**

sunlight

It stopped raining, and the sun came out. The
sunlight made everything bright! ▶ *noun*

sure

Are you **sure** you want to take such a long hike?
▶ *adjective* **sure, surer, surest**

Tt

talk

I like to **talk** to my grandmother
on the telephone.
▶ *verb* **talk, talking, talked**

tall

I am a metre **tall**. How **tall** are you?
▶ *adjective* **tall, taller, tallest**

taste

Grandma let us **taste** the pie she baked.
▶ *verb* **taste, tasting, tasted**

teeth

I brushed my **teeth** after each meal.
▶ *noun* **tooth, teeth**

tell

I want to **tell** you a secret.
▶ *verb* **tell, telling, told**

than

My house is nearer to school **than** yours is.

that

Can you hand me **that** book?

them

Call your sisters and ask **them** if they want to eat.

then

First we will draw a shape. **Then** we will cut it out.
Opposite **now**

there

Do you see the rose over **there** by the fence?

these

These are mine. Those are yours.

think

When I add numbers, I have to **think** carefully.
▶ *verb* **think, thinking, thought**

this

Look at **this** book. **This** is my favourite story.

three

Two and one more is **three**. ▶ *noun*

threw

The boy **threw** the ball to the girl. She caught it.
▶ *verb* **throw, throwing, threw, thrown**

throw

Throw the ball high, and I will catch it.
▶ *verb* **throw, throwing, threw, thrown**

Spelling Dictionary

Thursday
Every **Thursday** my uncle picks me up from school.
▶ *noun* **Thursday, Thursdays**

tight
These gloves are too **tight**. I need bigger ones.
▶ *adjective* **tight, tighter, tightest**

time
We spend a lot of **time** in school.
▶ *noun* **time, times**

toad
I saw a **toad** in the garden.
▶ *noun* **toad, toads**

toast
For breakfast, I have **toast** with jam.
▶ *noun*

today
Today is my birthday. *Opposite* **yesterday**

told
Mom **told** me a secret. She **told** me not to tell anyone. ▶ *verb* **tell, telling, told**

tomatoes
Dad picked the red, ripe **tomatoes**.
▶ *noun* **tomato, tomatoes**

too
She is going to soccer practice. I want to go, **too**.

took
Yesterday I **took** my brother to see a play.
▶ *verb* **take, taking, took, taken**

tooth
My **tooth** fell out yesterday. A new one will grow in. ▶ *noun* **tooth, teeth**

town
The **town** I live in is Kingston. What is your **town**? ▶ *noun* **town, towns**

troll

The fairy tale was about a mean **troll**.
▶ *noun* **troll, trolls**

true

This story really happened. It is a **true** story.
▶ *adjective* **true, truer, truest**

tube

Toothpaste comes in a **tube**. ▶ *noun* **tube, tubes**

Tuesday

I went to gym on **Tuesday**.
▶ *noun* **Tuesday, Tuesdays**

twins

My brother and I were born on the same day.
We are **twins**. ▶ *noun* **twin, twins**

two

I saw **two** birds fly by.
▶ *adjective*

Uu

up

Look **up** to see the moon.
Opposite **down**

upon

The boys came **upon** a hidden treasure.

us

We are hiding. No one can see **us**.

use

Your pencil is broken. You can **use** mine.
▶ *verb* **use, using, used**

Vv

very

It rained all month. We had **very** wet weather.

view

The **view** from my window is beautiful. I can see the mountains. ▶ *noun* **view, views**

wake

The baby is sleeping. Don't **wake** her.
▶ *verb* **wake, waking, woke, waked, woken**

walk

I like to take the bus to school, but my sister likes to **walk**. ▶ *verb* **walk, walking, walked**

wall

We hung a picture on the **wall**.
▶ *noun* **wall, walls**

was

Yesterday I **was** at home all day.
▶ *verb* **be, is, am, are, was, were, being, been**

Wednesday

Wednesday comes in the middle of the week.
▶ *noun* **Wednesday, Wednesdays**

week

There are seven days in a **week**.
▶ *noun* **week, weeks**

weekday

Monday is a **weekday**. So is Friday.
▶ *noun* **weekday, weekdays**

weekend

Saturday and Sunday are days of the **weekend**.
▶ *noun* **weekend, weekends**

well

I can paint **well**. I am very good at it.

went

Everyone **went** to the basketball game.
▶ *noun* **go, goes, going, went, gone**

whale

I saw a **whale** in the ocean.
▶ *noun* **whale, whales**

what

What is in your pocket?

wheel

I can't ride my bike. The back **wheel** is broken.
▶ *noun* **wheel, wheels**

when

When does school start? At nine o'clock!

where

I play at the park. **Where** do you play?

which

This coat is mine. **Which** one is yours?

while

Let's stop and rest for a **while**.

whisper

Listen! I will **whisper** a secret in your ear.
▶ *verb* **whisper, whispering, whispered**

whistle

If I **whistle**, the dog will come.
▶ *verb* **whistle, whistling, whistled**

white

The clean snow was **white**.
▶ *adjective* **white, whiter, whitest**

who

Who is out on the playground? Is anyone there?

whole

I ate the **whole** sandwich. None of it is left.
▶ *adjective*

whose

Whose shoes are these? They are my mom's.

window

When I look out my **window**, I see a tree. ▶ *noun* **window, windows**

wintertime
We wear warm coats in the **wintertime**. ▶ *noun*

wish
I blew out the candles and made a **wish**. I hope it comes true! ▶ *noun* **wish, wishes**

wishes
Some people make **wishes** when they see a star. ▶ *noun* **wish, wishes**

with
I will sit **with** you at lunch.

without
I was in a hurry. I left home **without** my lunchbox.

woman
The **woman** with me is my aunt. ▶ *noun* **woman, women**

women
Those three **women** look like sisters. ▶ *noun* **woman, women**

wood
The house is made of **wood**. The **wood** is from pine trees. ▶ *noun*

would
Would you like to share this orange? ▶ *verb* **will, would**

write
I like to **write** letters to my friends. ▶ *verb* **write, writing, wrote, written**

Yy

yellow
What colour is a lemon? It is **yellow**. ▶ *adjective*

yes
Will you come with me? **Yes**, I will. *Opposite* **no**

A a

B b

C c

D d

E e

F f

G g

H h

I i

Jj

Kk

Ll

M m

N n

O o

P p

Q q

R r

S s

T t

U u

V v

W w

X x

Y y

Z z